Grazer Philosophische Studien, Volume 92 – 2

Grazer Philosophische Studien

INTERNATIONAL JOURNAL FOR ANALYTIC PHILOSOPHY

Founded by

Rudolf Haller

Edited by

Johannes L. Brandl (*Universität Salzburg*)
Marian David (*Universität Graz*)
Maria E. Reicher (*Universität Aachen*)
Leopold Stubenberg (*University of Notre Dame*)

Managing Editor

Martina Fürst (*Universität Graz*)

Editorial Board

Peter Baumann – Monika Betzler – Elke Brendel – Annalisa Coliva
Victor Caston – Thomas Crisp – Katalin Farkas – Dagfinn Føllesdal
Volker Gadenne – Christopher Gauker – Hanjo Glock – Kathrin Glüer-Pagin
Robert M. Harnish † – Katherine Hawley – Christoph Jäger – Tom Kelly
Jaegwon Kim – Peter Koller – Nikola Kompa – Wolfgang Künne
Martin Kusch – Karel Lambert – Sandra Lapointe – Keith Lehrer
Hannes Leitgeb – Joseph Levine – Georg Meggle – Thomas Mormann
Edgar Morscher – Herlinde Pauer-Studer – Christian Piller – Marga Reimer
Tobias Rosefeldt – Edmund Runggaldier – Carolina Satorio – Werner Sauer
Susanna Schellenberg – Hans-Bernhard Schmid – Benjamin Schnieder
Gerhard Schurz – Geo Siegwart – Peter Simons – Barry Smith
Thomas Spitzley – Matthias Steup – Mark Textor – Udo Thiel – Thomas Uebel
Maria van der Schaar – Ted Warfield – Charlotte Werndl – Nicholas White

VOLUME 92

The titles published in this series are listed at *brill.com/gps*

Grazer Philosophische Studien
Volume 92 – 2015

International Journal for Analytic Philosophy

BRILL
RODOPI

LEIDEN | BOSTON

Grazer Philosophische Studien is published with the support of:
The Faculty of Humanities of the University of Graz and

Library of Congress Control Number: 2015955983

ISSN 0165-9227
ISBN 978-90-04-31083-4 (paperback)
ISBN 978-90-04-31084-1 (e-book)

Copyright 2015 by Koninklijke Brill NV, Leiden, The Netherlands.
Koninklijke Brill NV incorporates the imprints Brill, Brill Hes & De Graaf, Brill Nijhoff, Brill Rodopi and Hotei Publishing.
All rights reserved. No part of this publication may be reproduced, translated, stored in a retrieval system, or transmitted in any form or by any means, electronic, mechanical, photocopying, recording or otherwise, without prior written permission from the publisher.
Authorization to photocopy items for internal or personal use is granted by Koninklijke Brill NV provided that the appropriate fees are paid directly to The Copyright Clearance Center, 222 Rosewood Drive, Suite 910, Danvers, MA 01923, USA.
Fees are subject to change.

This book is printed on acid-free paper.

Printed by Printforce, the Netherlands

INHALTSVERZEICHNIS　　　　　　　　TABLE OF CONTENTS

Andrew LUGG: Wittgenstein on Colour Exclusion: Not Fatally Mistaken 1
Philip A. EBERT: Dummett's Criticism of the Context Principle 23
Nils KÜRBIS: What is Wrong with Classical Negation? 51
Ernâni MAGALHÃES: Plain Particulars 87
Ari MAUNU: Frege and the Description Theory: An Attempt at Rehabilitation 109

Essay-Wettbewerb　　　　　　　　*Essay Competition*

Dorothee BLEISCH: Die Moralpille – Über Risiken und Nebenwirkungen denken Sie eigenständig nach und fragen Ihren Philosophen oder Ihre Philosophin 117
Philip FOX: Agency & the Pill that Makes us Moral 127
David HEERING: Breaking Good: Is there a Patent Recipe for Cooking up the Moral Pill? 137

Buchnotizen　　　　　　　　　　*Critical Notes*

Wolfgang KÜNNE, *Epimenides und andere Lügner*. Frankfurt am Main: Klostermann Verlag, 2013 (Elke BRENDEL) 147
Denis FISETTE & Guillaume FRÉCHETTE (eds.), *Themes from Brentano*. Amsterdam-New York: Rodopi, 2013 (Fred KROON)　　152

WITTGENSTEIN ON COLOUR EXCLUSION:
NOT FATALLY MISTAKEN

Andrew LUGG
University of Ottawa

Abstract

The problem of colour exclusion is not fatal to Ludwig Wittgenstein's early philosophy, nor was it the catalyst for his later philosophy. His remarks in the *Tractatus* about the impossibility of the simultaneous occurrence of two colours at a point in the visual field sit comfortably with what he says in the rest of the book, his discussion of mathematical physics above all. Furthermore his second thoughts about the impossibility were a consequence, not the cause, of the turn his philosophy subsequently took.

Keywords: Ludwig Wittgenstein; colour exclusion problem; *Tractatus*; logical and mathematical representation; 'Some Remarks on Logical Form'; Russell; Ramsey; Hintikka & Hintikka

Ludwig Wittgenstein is generally held to have stumbled badly in 1916/1917 when discussing the impossibility of two colours occurring at the same place at the same time and held to have moved towards his later philosophy in 1929 on realising he had stumbled. The solution to the problem of colour exclusion he sketches in 6.3751 of the *Tractatus Logico-Philosophicus* is deemed ruinous for the book, and his belated appreciation of the point reckoned responsible for his dismantling the philosophy of the book and his developing the philosophy of the *Philosophical Investigations*. As a leading commentator has it: "The programme implicit in 6.3751 was to show that when '*A* is red' is fully analysed into its constituents, its truth will perspicuously entail that *A* is not blue", a programme later rejected on the grounds that "A is red and A is blue" is "not a simple logical *contradiction*, to be revealed as such by *analysis*, but a *nonsense*" (Hacker 1986, 108f.). I first consider what Wittgenstein says about colour exclusion in the *Tractatus*, then tackle the question of what set him on the path to the *Philosophical Investigations*. Mainly I aim to show that Wittgenstein was on firm ground in 1916/1917 and it was not the problem of colour exclusion but other considerations that prompted him in 1929 to rethink what he had earlier written, considerations that led to his revising his explanation of colour exclusion.

The received view of the treatment of colour exclusion in the *Tractatus* is not without basis in the text. In the third of the three paragraphs Wittgenstein devotes to the topic, he observes that while conjunctions of elementary propositions are never contradictions, conjunctions of propositions attributing different colours to a point in the visual field always are. He writes (within parentheses): "It is clear that the logical product [conjunction] of two elementary propositions [*Elementarsätze*] can neither be a tautology nor a contradiction. The assertion that a point in the visual field has two different colours at the same time, is a contradiction" (1922, 6.3751). From this, it follows—*Elementarsätze* being logically independent and contradictory propositions being invariably false—that propositions about the colours of points in the visual field are complex, not elementary. In other words, just as the conventional wisdom has it, Wittgenstein holds that assertions to the effect that a point in the visual field has two colours are not conjunctions of elementary propositions (presumably if either conjunct is elementary, so is the other). As Wittgenstein puts it in material he drew on when drafting 6.3751: "If the logical product of two propositions is a contradiction and the propositions appear to be elementary propositions, we can see that in this case the appearance is deceptive. (E.g.: A is red and A is green)" (1979, 91).

This line of thought was not a last minute addition reasonably ignored. The discussion of colour exclusion in the *Tractatus* derives from remarks composed some time before the book was compiled, and there is every reason to think Wittgenstein was satisfied with what he says at 6.3751. He recycles remarks in the *Prototractatus* penned in 1917/1918 practically verbatim, remarks that distil entries in *Notebooks 1914-1916* dated 16 August 1916 and 8 January 1917 (1971, 6.3751–6.3752 and 1979, 81, 91/2000, MS 104, 88, 94). Had he come to doubt his treatment of the problem, he would surely have reworked his earlier remarks, not reproduced them with very small changes and minor omissions. (The only noteworthy difference is that in the last version of the material he speaks of points in the visual field instead of points as having two colours.) Nor can his remarks on the topic be regarded as incidental to his discussion. He could not duck the task of accounting for the contradictory character of "A is red and A is green" given his view that "[t]here is only *logical* necessity" (6.37). And he was in no position either to forego the principle that elementary propositions are logically independent, this being central to his thinking as a whole, not just to the discussion of 6.3751 (compare 4.211 and 5.134).

To clarify the difficulty that is alleged to bedevil the treatment of colour exclusion in the *Tractatus*, it helps to consider Wittgenstein's treatment of the example of a point—or point in the visual field—that is simultaneously both red and green. On the one hand the conclusion that "A is red" and "A is green" cannot be elementary is deemed "unwelcome" since the attribution of a colour to a point is "close to our conception of what an elementary proposition ought to be like" (Black 1964, 367f.). On the other hand it is noted that "A is red" and "A is green" cannot be complex since an analysis of them in terms, say, of "surface reflectance potentials" would only shift the problem to one of explaining "the impossibility of a particle (photon) having different velocities at the same time" (Landini 2007, 87). Simply put, if the attribution of two colours to a single point in the visual field at the same time is contradictory, the attribution of a colour to such a point, regarded either as elementary or as non-elementary, cannot be accommodated within the framework of the *Tractatus*, and it is only puzzling that Wittgenstein took so long to see the problem and come up with a solution.

Though widely endorsed, this objection to what Wittgenstein says about colour exclusion in the *Tractatus* is not conclusive. Wittgenstein does, it is true, write in the *Notebooks 1914–1916*: "As examples of simples I always think of points in the visual field (just as parts of the visual field always come before my mind as typical composite objects)" (1979, 45, dated 6 May 1915). This by itself, however, does not show he rejected the conclusion that "A is red" is analysable. For one thing, right after confessing that he thinks of points in the visual field as simples, he asks: "But what is a uniformly coloured part of my visual field composed of? Of *minima sensibilia*?" (1979, 45, dated 7 May 1915; also compare 1979, 64, dated 18 June 1915, and 1979, 67, dated 20 June 1915). And for another thing, between writing these remarks and compiling the *Tractatus* he may well have come to think that, however "unwelcome", the fact that "A is red and A is green" is a contradiction shows that the attribution of a colour to a point cannot be elementary. It is even possible that he set down the material that became the third paragraph of 6.3751 some months after drafting the material that became the other two paragraphs for the express purpose of signalling that "A is red" and "A is green" should be regarded as non-elementary, their conjunction being "a contradiction".

And it is unlikely as well that Wittgenstein would have been swayed by the objection that it only defers the problem to regard attributions of colours to points as non-elementary. Had he believed "A is red" is analysable in terms of positions, velocities, wavelengths, surface reflectance potentials or the like, he would, no two ways about it, have left himself open to the charge of putting off the evil day. But it is difficult to credit that he missed that an analysis of such propositions in more basic terms would be beset by a similar, if not an identical, problem. It is, moreover, quite wrong to read him, as he has been repeatedly read, as intimating in the second paragraph of 6.3751—oblivious of just how little this would achieve—that attributions of colours to points are analysable in spatio-temporal terms. In this paragraph he confines himself to noting a comparable case. "Let us", he says, "consider how this contradiction presents itself in physics: Somewhat as follows: That a particle cannot at the same time have two velocities, *i.e.* that at the same time it cannot be in two places, *i.e.* that particles in different places at the same time cannot be identical". This is not to say "A is red and A is green" is analysable in physical terms, only to observe that there are similar contradictions in physics, "X is at two positions" and "X has two velocities", for instance.

The burden of Wittgenstein's remarks in the third paragraph of 6.3751 is that the attribution of a colour to a point in the visual field is analysable in a manner consistent with the fact that attributing two colours to a point is a "contradiction" (and the conception of elementary propositions as logically independent). In the *Tractatus* non-reductive analysis is extolled (compare 4.0031, 5.532–5.5321), and Wittgenstein would not, I conjecture, have balked at the idea that assertions about the joint occurrence of colours are subject to this sort of analysis. While reductive analyses in terms of physical or other more basic notions may only relocate the problem, nonreductive analyses, which remain at the same level as the original assertion, plainly need not. "Area A in the visual field has at least one blemish and is without blemish" is analysable as "There is a blemish that A has, and it is false that there is a blemish that A has", and it is not out of the question that contradictions of the sort referred to at 6.3751 are subject to comparable—if more complex—analysis. While there is no guarantee that "A is red and A is green" can be re-expressed as a formal contradiction stating that something both is and is not the case, neither is it impossible that Wittgenstein had something of the kind in mind.

It is also of no little consequence that Wittgenstein seems to have been unfazed by the objection that an analysis of "A is red and A is green" would get us no further ahead. He would have known that Frank Ramsey had argued just this as early as 1923, indeed written in a review of the *Tractatus*: "Mr Wittgenstein is only reducing the difficulty to that of the *necessary* properties of space, time, and matter or the ether", properties "hardly capable of further reduction of this kind" (Ramsey 1923, 473). Whether or not Wittgenstein read Ramsey's review, he would doubtless have heard of the objection from Ramsey himself, it being scarcely credible that it was not mentioned when Ramsey visited him in Austria some months after writing the review and they went through the *Tractatus* remark-by-remark. In the event it seems to have been Ramsey, not Wittgenstein, who ended up persuaded he had things wrong. Ramsey never subsequently pressed the objection, and when he hazarded his own explanation of colour exclusion in 1927, he allowed that "formal logic … presupposes that the truth-possibilities of atomic sentences are possible", declared that the self-contradictoriness of "This is both blue and red" is "concealed by a defective analysis" and compared the contradiction with a "mechanically impossible" situation (1990, 48).

Equally significantly, Bertrand Russell passes over the topic of colour exclusion in silence in the "Introduction" he wrote for the *Tractatus*. Were Wittgenstein's discussion of colour exclusion at 6.3751 as flawed as regularly charged, it is hard to imagine Russell, who had a nose for philosophical gaffes second to none, not spotting and commenting on the fact. While his saying nothing is no guarantee that he agreed with Wittgenstein on the question of how the likes of "A is red and A is green" are to be understood, his saying nothing provides some reason for thinking he did not reject Wittgenstein's thinking out of hand. In his "Introduction" he points out what he takes to be defects in the *Tractatus*, some large, some small, seemingly without a moment's hesitation, and it is unlikely he would have refrained from noting so big a defect, if such it be, along with the others. Since this would have meant him pulling punches to an unusual degree, the safest assumption would appear to be that in his eyes Wittgenstein had not blundered terribly. It is even reasonable, given the tenor of his "Introduction", to conclude that Russell found Wittgenstein's explanation of colour exclusion to be, if not entirely adequate, very nearly so.

This assumption deserves sympathetic consideration especially as the discussion of colour exclusion in the *Tractatus* echoes the discussion of the topic in Russell's *Principles of Mathematics*, a work Wittgenstein had studied closely (Landini 2007, 86–88 and Lugg 2015). Wittgenstein reprises—one could say appropriates—Russell's view that the impossibility is to be traced to the essential nature of colour, the sole difference between his treatment of the problem and Russell's being that he traces the impossibility to "the logical structure of colour" (1922, 6.3751, first paragraph), Russell to a "fundamental characteristic of matter" (1903, 467). While Wittgenstein does not refer to "impenetrability", the characteristic of matter that Russell takes to show that "no two colours can be in the same place at once", he agrees that two colours occurring together is logically excluded. And it is also striking that Wittgenstein follows Russell in the second paragraph of 6.3751 when he draws attention to the occurrence of similar contradictions in physics, Russell having already mentioned in the *Principles* that colour exclusion is similar to mechanical impossibility (1903, 473). No wonder, then, that Wittgenstein does not go into detail and Russell says nothing about 6.3751. Both of them would have taken the problem to have been already taken care of.

Wittgenstein's solution of the problem occurs in the first paragraph of 6.3751, a paragraph much less examined than the other two. It is, I believe, insufficiently recognised that in this paragraph Wittgenstein, following in Russell's footsteps, provides an explanation of colour exclusion that is immune to criticism of the sort generally taken to put paid to the argument of the *Tractatus*. Far from simply ignoring the question of what prevents two colours occurring simultaneous at the same point in the visual field at the same time, he observes that this is impossible because of the nature of colour itself. Summarising his thinking, he writes: "For two colours, *e.g.* to be at one place in the visual field, is impossible, logically impossible, for it is excluded by the logical structure of colour [*logische Struktur der Farbe*]". By this he means the occurrence of two colours at a point is logically ruled out by our concept of colour or, what for him is the same, by how colour is thought and spoken about. Nothing can be simultaneously red and green all over, he would have us recognise, because it is essential to colour—i.e. integral to the logic of colour concepts—that occurrences of red exclude occurrences of green and *vice versa*.

When the first paragraph of 6.3751 is seen as providing Wittgenstein's leading idea, the second paragraph poses no special problem. There is no hiatus between his claiming that two colours cannot be at the same point in the visual field because of the logical structure of colour and his observing that "this contradiction presents itself in physics". He is simply noting that colour exclusion is matched by position and velocity exclusion and points in the visual field can no more have two colours given the logical structure of colour than particles can have two positions or two velocities given the logical structure of matter and motion, i.e. in the one case as in the other the impossibility is logical, not empirical. In fact in *Notebooks 1914–1916* Wittgenstein compares the impossibility of a point of more than one colour with the impossibility of a particle at more than one place, which is excluded by "the structure of space and of particles" (1979, 81). While "a particle cannot be in two places at the same time does look more like a logical impossibility", he writes, the impossibility of a point having two colours at the same time is ruled out by how we conceive the world, not by how the world happens to be, the reason being that "the very language of physics reduces it to a kinetic [i.e. mathematical] impossibility".

The account of colour exclusion in 6.3751 that emerges when the spotlight is shone on the first paragraph of the number rather than the other two is thus very different from the standard account. It is no mystery why Wittgenstein would have believed he had answered the question and found Ramsey's criticism unpersuasive, perhaps even why Ramsey did not repeat his objection after visiting Wittgenstein in 1923. In the *Tractatus* colour is regarded, like matter and motion, as logically structured, and colour exclusion taken, along with position and velocity exclusion, to be logically instead of empirically or metaphysically impossible. For Wittgenstein colour attributions, position attributions and velocity attributions can all be analysed in a way that brings out the contradictory character of the "impossibilities". Moreover he gives the impression that he took such analyses to conform to the argument of the rest of the book, not least to the account of logic he provides. But if so, how exactly did he understand the all-important notion of "the logical structure of colour" and how did he imagine—given how he construes logic—that he could show the joint occurrence of red and green is logically excluded by appealing to this notion?

Wittgenstein does not tackle this question explicitly in the *Tractatus*. There are in the book, however, hints as to how he would have answered it had he been challenged. At 2.0131 he implies that red, yellow, green, blue and the rest are logically interrelated inasmuch as the relationships of entailment and inconsistency among colours mirror the relationships of entailment and inconsistency among points in "colour space". He writes: "A speck in a visual field need not be red but it must have a colour; it has, so to speak, a colour space [*Farbenraum*] around it" (also 1971, 2.0142). Nor can it be by chance that he placed the discussion of colour exclusion in the part of the *Tractatus* devoted to mathematical physics, material in which the notion of a space of possibilities looms large. He is best understood as going along with Russell and taking his account of mathematical physics to extend—with trivial revisions and qualifications—to colour, i.e. as holding that colour is no less mathematically representable than matter and motion. Most charitably read, he was of the opinion that our system of colour concepts, like mechanics, determines "a form of description", one akin to a grid or network ("*Netz*") (1922, 6.341). In his view it too "is *purely* geometrical, and all its properties can be given a priori" (6.35; also 1979, 38).

The conception of mathematical representation was deep in Wittgenstein's thinking. Possibly as a result of his training in science, possibly as a result of his own early reading, he viewed qualities and quantities in the manner favoured by mathematical physicists and by all appearances regarded colour along with position and velocity as representable by points in abstract spaces of possibilities. Ludwig Boltzmann and Heinrich Hertz are the first two thinkers on the list of influences Wittgenstein drew up in 1930 (1998, 16), and their way of representing phenomena underlies his reflections on language and the world. It is unmistakable that in his discussion of Newtonian Mechanics (1979, 35; 1922, 6.341) he is working with what Hertz variously calls "representations of the principles of mechanics", "modes of expression" and "modes of representation" (1899, 4, 9, 24). And it cannot be fortuitous either that in *Notebooks 1914–1916* he says—just before referring to Hertz's "invisible masses"—he has "felt for a *long* time" that mechanics is a form of description (1979, 36, dated 6 December 1914). Moreover in the *Tractatus* itself he alludes to "Hertz's Mechanics, on Dynamic Models" (4.04) and expresses his thinking at one point in "the terminology of Hertz" (6.361). (Also I fancy Wittgenstein would have been familiar with Russell's account of Hertz's dynamics in Chapter LIX of the *Principles*.)

When Wittgenstein is understood as construing representation mathematically and equating the logical structure of colour with the geometry of colour space, his treatment of colour exclusion is readily understood. To his way of thinking, it is no more puzzling than position exclusion, specks in the visual field being associated with one and only one colour in colour space just as particles are associated with one and only one position in Euclidean space (and the squares of a net being either empty or filled). Given that different colours are represented by different points in colour space, it immediately follows that specks can have no more than one colour and "A is red" and "A is green" cannot be true together. Just as the logical structure of matter and motion (and "[t]he form of description" associated with Newtonian mechanics) entails that particles are located at one and only one position, so the logical structure of colour (and the form of description associated with our system of colour concepts) entails that specks in the visual field have one and only one colour. A "form of description", whether for colour or matter and motion, defines what can and cannot be sensibly said and hence defines what is logically "excluded [*ausgeschlosse*n]" (6.3751).

The suggestion that Wittgenstein embraces the Hertz/Boltzmann mathematical conception of representation when explaining colour exclusion is further bolstered by the fact that he takes phenomena, without any apparent reluctance, to be representable by their coordinates (compare locating a city by means of its latitude and longitude). In a remark composed early on he writes: "We might conceive two co-ordinates a_p and b_p as a proposition stating that the material point P is to be found in the place (ab)" (1979, 20, dated 29 October 1914), and it is beyond belief that he regarded the attribution of colour to a point any differently. On this conception there is no asserting that a point can be red and green simultaneously since there is no coordinate corresponding to both "A is red" and "A is green". The assertion that a point in visual space is correlated with two distinct coordinates in colour space is as absurd as the assertion that a material point is correlated with both $(a_1 b_1)$ and $(a_2 b_2)$ in geometrical space (compare stating that a city has more than one latitude and longitude). As Wittgenstein says: "It is no more possible to present something 'contradicting logic' in language than to present a figure contradicting the laws of space in geometry by means of its co-ordinates; or, say, to give the co-ordinates of a point that does not exist" (1979, 40, dated 16 May 1915; also 1922, 3.032).

If qualities and quantities are representable by points in a multi-dimensional space, attributions of colours to points are representable in functional terms. "[T]he general concept of colour can", as has been noted, "be represented in language, not by a class of colour-predicates, but by a function c which maps points in visual space into a colour space" (Hintikka and Hintikka 1986, 123). (Compare the "height"-function which associates people with their heights.) Adopting this conception of representation, "A is red" is symbolised as "$c(A) = r$" (where "r" designates red) rather than as "Ra" (where "R" holds a place for "is red"). And likewise "A is green" is symbolised as "$c(A) = g$" (where "g" designates green) rather than as "Ga" (where "G" holds a place for "is green"). Whence since "a function cannot have two different values for the same argument", it can be inferred without further ado that "the two propositions are *logically* incompatible". In other words "c(a) = r & c(a) = g" is logically excluded for the simple reason that the colour function, c, always returns a single value in colour space for each argument in visual (or speck) space. The only remaining question is whether Wittgenstein had this explanation of the impossibility in mind when he wrote the *Tractatus*.

This may be doubted as "the historical truth seems to be that Wittgenstein never says he is construing colour functionally" and "it may very well turn out that he never assented to it verbally" (Hintikka and Hintikka 1986, 124). But even granting Wittgenstein neither said nor assented to it, it seems wrong to conclude that "the most that we can claim here is that the construal of colour as a function mapping points in visual space into colour space is in keeping with the spirit of [his] thinking". Leaving aside the possibility that he deployed the construal without a second thought (or considered it too commonplace to belabour), he is **most** plausibly read as committed to the construal in the *Tractatus*. At 2.0131 (and 1971, 2.01411), he not only observes that specks in the visual field are surrounded by "a colour space", he also writes: "A spatial object must lie in infinite space. (A point in space is an argument place)". Given this view—that objects are functionally related to positions—it would have been remarkable had he not also regarded specks as functionally related to colours, the one as "arguments", the other as "values". Moreover if it is "forcefully asserted" at 2.0131 that "attributions of different perceptual qualities are … represented logically speaking by genuine functions", why regard the mapping construal of colour as merely a "thought experiment" (Hintikka and Hintikka 1986, 123)?

To argue that Wittgenstein's discussion of colour exclusion in the *Tractatus* accords well with his remarks about colour space and mathematical physics does not, however, show he is out of the woods. In the first paragraph of 6.3751 he refers to "the logical structure of colour", not to its mathematical structure. In the second paragraph he speaks of "this contradiction" rather than this mathematical impossibility as arising in physics. And in the third paragraph he states that the assertion that a point in the visual field has two different colours is "a contradiction", not that it is mathematically inconsistent. One might even be forgiven for thinking that I have unwittingly demonstrated that Wittgenstein is in a deeper hole than generally supposed, his discussion of mathematics and mathematical physics being equally at variance with what he says in the rest of the book. If his account of colour exclusion goes hand in hand with his account of mathematics and mathematical physics, is not the major difficulty alleged to plague the *Tractatus* exacerbated rather than put to rest? Wittgenstein cannot, it may well be argued, have been committed to treating representation like Hertz and Boltzmann without cutting himself off from treating representation, as he certainly did, like Frege and Russell.

The trouble that I see with this is that it wrongly presumes that Wittgenstein believed mathematical representation is irreducible to logical representation whereas in fact he regarded the two conceptions of representation as going together and took mathematical impossibility to be of a piece with logically impossibility. The most reasonable hypothesis is that he believed Russell had shown that mathematics is in essence logic and following on from this had concluded that it is logically impossible—since mathematically impossible—for a point to have two colours simultaneously. By all indications, he accepted that by specifying "the kinematical conditions for a system of material particles, generalized and expressed in terms of logical constants", Russell had provided an "abstract logical statement of what rational Dynamics requires its matter to be" (1903, 468). Wittgenstein does not, as commonly believed, challenge Russell on the relationship of mathematics to logic but accepts that he had shown that "[t]he à priori truths involved in Dynamics are only those of logic" (488), indeed managed to establish "the logical nature of mathematics … throughout" (498). As he saw it, any residual errors in Russell's discussion are remediable without materially compromising his own treatment of mathematics, mathematical physics and colour exclusion.

The main snag with this defence of Wittgenstein's argument in the *Tractatus* would seem to be that it fails to take into account that he construes logical propositions very differently from mathematical propositions. It is taken as gospel that he differs from Russell regarding the relationship of mathematics to logic since he explicitly says: "The propositions of logic are tautologies" (1922, 6.1). This does not, however, mean he remains on the hook, there being ample reason to think he did not regard tautologies as narrowly as they are nowadays regarded. The present-day notion of tautology was not in place in the early decades of the twentieth century, and Wittgenstein mostly worked with the traditional notion of tautologies as propositions that convey no information (compare 4.461, 5.142, 6.11; also Dreben and Floyd 1991 and Lugg 2003 and 2013). In this regard it bears underlining that Russell did not hesitate to write some years after writing his "Introduction" that "[t]he propositions which form part of logic, or can be proved by logic, are all *tautologies*" and "all pure mathematics consists of tautologies in [this] sense" (1927, 171). And still more tellingly Ramsey maintained around the same time that "mathematics consists of tautologies" (1990, 176) and referred to the Multiplicative Axiom (i.e. the axiom of choice) as "an obvious tautology" (1990, 222).

These historical observations notwithstanding, it may be argued that in the *Tractatus* Wittgenstein identifies logic with what is nowadays referred to as predicate logic (if not just sentence logic), a system of logic much too weak to encompass mathematics. There is, I imagine it being objected, no escaping the fact that mathematical propositions cannot be obtained, as Wittgenstein claims all propositions can be obtained, from a base of elementary propositions by successive application of the "N-operator", the operator that yields the conjunction of the negations of a given set of propositions (5.5 and 6). In response, I would point out that Wittgenstein actually had a conception of logic close, if not equal, in expressive power to logic as Russell conceived it. At 5.501 he mentions three ways of forming propositions, the first covering sentence logic, the second predicate logic and the third higher-order logic, a system strong enough to retrieve at least a fair amount of mathematics (compare Ricketts 2013, 129–139). While 5.501 and other remarks that suggest that Wittgenstein had a rich conception of logic (e.g. 3.331 and 4.1273) require interpretation and it is debatable how much mathematics he could justifiably be said to recover, there can be no denying that he took logic to comprise more than the tautologies of sentence and predicate logic.

All this notwithstanding, Wittgenstein may be thought at odds with Russell since he holds that mathematics is categorically different from logic. The most important obstacle to what I am urging would seem to be that in the *Tractatus* Wittgenstein eschews Russell's view of mathematics as an extension of logic when he writes: "The propositions of logic are tautologies. ... The propositions of mathematics are equations [*Gleichungen*]" (6.1 and 6.2). None of this can be gainsaid but neither is it conclusive. Wittgenstein does not state straight-out that mathematics falls in a different category from logic but rather comments on the two endeavours. For him mathematics is "a logical method [*eine logische Methode*]" (1922, 6.2), "a method of logic [*eine Methode der Logik*]" (6.234), and "[t]he equation characterises the standpoint from which I consider the two expressions, that is to say the standpoint of their equality of meaning [*Bedeutungsgleicheit*]" (6.2323). While these remarks require interpretation and scarcely prove that Wittgenstein did not repudiate Russell's view that mathematics is in essence logic, they show that the easy assumption that they differed substantially over the question of whether mathematics is reducible to logic leaves something to be desired (also compare Friedman 1999, 182f.).

In favour of the present way of understanding Wittgenstein on mathematics, it is also worth noting that in the *Tractatus* he is concerned with the general question of the nature of mathematics, not with the technical question of its reducibility to logic. In 6.02–6.031, his first series of remarks on mathematics, he suggests that numbers can be generated by repeated application of the successor operation starting from zero in much the same way as propositions can be generated by repeated application of the N-operator. And in 6.2–6.241, his other series on the subject, he observes that mathematical propositions are like logical propositions in that they are "*Scheinsätze*" (6.2), say nothing (6.21), show "the logic of the world" (6.22), do not require anything by way of "intuition" for their proof beyond what "language itself … supplies" (6.233) and "must be self-evident" (6.2341). None of this runs counter to Russell's claim that mathematics is at root logic, a view that Russell himself seems to have agreed with. In his "Introduction", he notes that "[t]here are some respects, in which … Mr Wittgenstein's theory stands in need of greater technical development", especially "his theory of numbers", but he does not find "anything in Mr Wittgenstein's system that makes it impossible for him to fill this lacuna" (Wittgenstein 1922, 21).

Consideration of the background to Wittgenstein's remarks also suggests that his view of mathematics and logic is close to Russell's. Like most interested parties at the time, he was impressed by the argument that Russell (and Alfred North Whitehead) mounted in *Principia Mathematica* for regarding mathematics as essentially logic. What bothered him was not Russell's technical argument but his understanding and presentation of it. When compiling the *Tractatus*, Wittgenstein's chief interest remained —as David Pinsent, a close friend, described it in his diary on 25 August 1913—"the very fundamental part of the subject", not Russell's "purely Mathematical work—for instance most of his 'Principia'" (1990, 59). As a matter of fact Wittgenstein drafted the remarks on mathematics late in the day (2000, MS 104, 70 and 100–101, 117–118; 1971, 200 and 216–218), and one has the sense that he believed they could be smoothly grafted onto what he had written about logic in *Notebooks 1914–1916*. He seems to have had no compunction about recycling what he had earlier written about mathematics (and mathematical physics) pretty much word for word in the *Prototractatus* and the *Tractatus* after he had introduced the notion of an operation, sketched his "theory of number" and discussed the nature of mathematics. Nor should it be overlooked that in the *Prototractatus* he restates that the likes of "A is red and A is green" are contradictory after giving "[t]he general form of an integer" (2000, MS 104, 70 and 94; 1971, 229 and 203).

Turning now to the question of why Wittgenstein came to repudiate the discussion of colour exclusion in the *Tractatus*, this too calls for a different answer from the one typically offered. There is no indication that Wittgenstein came to believe he had erred at 6.3751 about the topic prior to 1929, when after some ten years engaged in other business, he started writing again on philosophy. During the period he was only minimally concerned with philosophy and there is no sign of his having recanted what he says in 6.3751, never mind his regarding it as dooming the philosophical vision promoted in the book. Nothing in the material that has come down to us indicates that he did not remain committed to the view that the joint occurrence of two colours at a point in the visual field is excluded by "the logical structure of colour" (and as comparable to position and velocity exclusion). But if he continued to go along, with minor reservations, with Russell's account of the phenomenon in the *Principles* and to hew to a Hertzian view of mathematical physics, what prompted him to revise his thinking about colour exclusion in the months following his return to philosophy? Nobody denies that he began in 1929 to dismantle the philosophy in the *Tractatus*. What is debatable is only how his thinking about colour exclusion contributed to bringing the house down.

Wittgenstein is standardly taken to have criticised the discussion of colour exclusion in the *Tractatus* in "Some Remarks on Logical Form", a paper he initially planned to deliver at the (British) Aristotelian Society in July 1929 (1993, 29–35). In this paper he is supposed to have targeted the thought advanced in the third paragraph of 6.3751 about the joint attribution of colours to a point in the visual field being contradictory. The contention is that "he stated clearly the inadequacy of the solution [to the problem of colour exclusion] in the *Tractatus*" and "tackled the issue head on" (Hacker 1986, 109). This is a simple and seemingly explanatory account of the development of Wittgenstein's thought. The only hitch is that it labours under considerable difficulty, and there is an alternative account, one in keeping with what I have suggested Wittgenstein says in the *Tractatus* and what he wrote in MS 105, the first surviving document from the period. As I understand the situation, his about-face was induced by considerations other than what he had written at 6.3751, considerations that convinced him that the attribution of a colour to a point in the visual field is elementary, not complex, and colour exclusion required a new explanation.

As often noted, Wittgenstein treats the impossibility of two colours at a point differently in "Some Remarks on Logical Form" from how he treats it in the *Tractatus*. Rather than claiming analysis reveals the assertion of two colours at a point to be formally contradictory, Wittgenstein writes in the fifth of the six paragraphs of the paper: "Our symbolism, which allows us to form the sign of the logical product of 'RPT' and 'BPT' [i.e. 'Colour R and colour B are at place P at time T'] gives no correct picture of reality" (1993, 34). He now regards the invariable falsity of "RPT & BPT" as traceable to the fact that "'( ) PT' leaves room only for one entity". Taking "RPT" and "BPT" to be "in a certain sense *complete*" (33) and "RPT & BPT" to lead to "collision" (34), he concludes that it is "a deficiency of our notation that it does not prevent the formation of such nonsensical constructions" (35). What is at stake regarding the question of the role of Wittgenstein's thinking about colour exclusion in the development of his philosophy, however, is not whether Wittgenstein believed "a perfect notation will exclude such structures by definite rules of syntax" but why he believed it. The crucial question is what persuaded him to regard "RPT" and "BPT" as "*complete*" and conclude that there have to be rules of syntax that "tell us that in the case of certain kinds of atomic propositions ... certain combinations of [truth possibilities] must be left out".

It is poorly appreciated, if appreciated at all, that there is no argument in "Some Remarks on Logical Form" for the conclusion that attributions of colours to points are elementary/atomic beyond the bare statement that "RPT" and "BPT" collide. In the fourth paragraph he notes in support of the view that "the statement which attributes a degree to a quality cannot be further analysed" (1993, 33) that "Entity E has two units of brightness" cannot be analysed either as "E has one unit of brightness and E has one unit of brightness" or as "E has b' and b'' units of brightness", the first analysis being logically equivalent to "E has one unit of brightness", the second leaving open the "obviously absurd" question of whether "E has one unit of brightness" is the same as "E has b' units of brightness" or "E has b'' units of brightness" (32f.). But this by itself hardly proves that statements of degree, let alone attributions of colours to points, are elementary. And how likely is it anyway that Wittgenstein believed "E has two units of brightness" is beyond the scope of the *Tractatus*? He knew as well as anyone that mechanics deals with degrees of qualities and would have regarded "two units of brightness" as no more problematic than "two units of momentum".

Since Wittgenstein says next to nothing in "Some Remarks on Logical Form" in support of treating "RPT" and "BPT" as elementary, it is highly unlikely he was out to establish the point. The least risky assumption is thus that in the fourth paragraph of the paper he is motivating the claim that atomic/elementary propositions may involve numbers, more specifically the claim, stated in the third paragraph, that "numbers will have to enter [the forms of elementary propositions] when—as we should say in ordinary language—we are dealing with properties which admit of gradation" (1993, 32). On this reading of Wittgenstein's remarks, it is a premise of his discussion, not a conclusion, that "the occurrence of numbers in the forms of atomic propositions is … not merely a feature of a special symbolism, but an essential and, consequently, unavoidable feature of [our way of representing phenomena]". He is presupposing rather than arguing for the view that when "we try to get at an actual analysis, we find logical forms that have very little similarity with the norms of ordinary language", in fact "meet with the forms of space and time with the whole manifold of spatial and temporal objects, as colours, sounds, etc., etc., with their gradations, continuous transitions, and combinations in various proportions" (31).

"Some Remarks on Logical Form" falls into two parts. In the first three paragraphs Wittgenstein announces that "[e]very proposition has a form and a content" (1993, 29), considers what analysis involves and the type of proposition it reveals (29–31) and floats the idea that an analysis of propositions uncovers the forms of space and time, colours and the like (31f.). Only then, in the remaining three paragraphs, does Wittgenstein discuss the problem of colour exclusion. What he says here rests on the unproven assumption that "numbers (rational and irrational) must enter into the structure of the atomic propositions themselves" (31). This crucial premise—Wittgenstein bills it as his "first definite remark on the logical analysis of actual phenomena"—is the pivot around which his discussion turns. Without it, his examination of the analysability of "RPT" and "BPT", an examination that is usually regarded as showing he had erred in the *Tractatus* about colour exclusion, is totally lacking in force. (It is, I am inclined to think, not a bad bet that it was Wittgenstein's "first definite remark" that inspired him to write "Some Remarks on Logical Form" and, given he does not defend the remark, why he attempted to withdraw the paper and spoke on another topic at the Aristotelian Society.)

So there was, as I see it, no failure of awareness on Wittgenstein's part in the *Tractatus* concerning the attribution of colours to points in the visual field and no acknowledgement in "Some Remarks on Logical Form" that there is something wrong with what he wrote about it in the book. He should not be criticised for missing something no thoughtful philosopher should have missed and for noticing that he had slipped up only very much later. The explanation of colour exclusion in the first paragraph of 6.3751 of the *Tractatus* is not easily rebutted, and Wittgenstein does not palm off "the most famous counter-example [to taking all necessity to be logical necessity] as an *illustration* of the thesis", explicable "only with reference to [his] vaunting confidence that the truth of his thoughts was 'unassailable and definitive'" (Fogelin 1987, 91-92). On the contrary, when he is read as going along with Russell regarding colour exclusion and accepting that mathematics is an extension of logic, he is seen to be fully justified in sticking with his earlier view of colour exclusion. More generously understood, he came to believe something else in the *Tractatus* is unsatisfactory, and it was this, not what he says at 6.3751, that led to his adopting the view of elementary propositions set out in "Some Remarks on Logical Form".

Granting that the common reading of Wittgenstein's 1929 paper gets things back to front and Wittgenstein developed a new account of the logical impossibility of the joint occurrence of colours after—rather than before—coming to think that rational and irrational numbers can figure in elementary propositions, what sent him back to the drawing board? No doubt one important factor was that in the early months of 1929 he "ceas[ed] to believe in the possibility of a truth-functional account of generality and the quantifiers" (White 2006, 140), this being something that he later referred to as a shortcoming of the *Tractatus* (e.g. 1979, 38–41). There also seems, however, to have been more to it (and not only because it is not immediately obvious why such a shortcoming would have caused him to turn his back on the explanation of colour exclusion offered in the *Tractatus*). More likely, it seems to me, his reflections on the nature of mathematics and the geometry of the visual field tipped the balance. While it is hard to say exactly what Wittgenstein was thinking during the months prior to his writing "Some Remarks on Logical Form", there is good circumstantial evidence that these reflections converted him to the view that numbers enter the form of elementary propositions, or at least were an important part of the mix.

On returning to Cambridge in January 1929 Wittgenstein was in regular conversation with Ramsey about mathematics, conversation that could not but have encouraged him (along with his own deliberations) to reconsider his earlier thinking about mathematical and logical representation. It is a reasonable conjecture that Ramsey told Wittgenstein that he had concluded, after working long and hard on the philosophy of mathematics adumbrated in the *Tractatus*, that it is "faced with insuperable difficulties" (1990, 180; published in 1925) and he was currently of the belief that "not merely some [of the terms of our language] but even all may be best symbolized by numbers", indeed that "colours have a structure, in which any given colour can be assigned a place by three numbers" (1990, 113; drafted in 1929). Such observations, assuming they were aired, would have made Wittgenstein think again about mathematics and colour attribution, not least whether he had—as he is later reported to have conceded—mistakenly treated "mathematics as a part of logic" (Waismann 1979, 218). In addition there is the striking fact that in what seem to be preparatory notes for his talk at the Aristotelian Society Wittgenstein takes an "intuition [*Anschauung*]" about mathematical infinity to entail that "there are no elementary propositions" (2010, 177).

It is also likely that Wittgenstein's thinking about the logical character of the visual field added fuel to the fire. As has been pointed out, "[t]he central theme of his reflections [in MS 105] is the logical analysis of the structure of the visual field" (Hacker 1986, 109), and "the numerical representation of the visual field is at the centre of [his writing on the topic]" (Engelmann 2103, 280, ftn 40). During the first months of 1929 Wittgenstein retains his earlier conception of an elementary proposition but sees that the geometry of visual space does not coincide in any straightforward way with the geometry of physical space, the only sort of geometry he had considered in the *Tractatus* (2000, MS 105, 1–3). This could not but have fostered the idea that the geometry of the visual field is in a class of its own and arithmetic belongs to the base of language, not only to its superstructure. There is, I picture Wittgenstein thinking, no avoiding the conclusion that numbers enter into the structure of elementary propositions, a conclusion that virtually duplicates the "first definite remark on the logical analysis of actual phenomena" in "Some Remarks on Logical Form".

Several remarks in MS 105 further support the hypothesis that Wittgenstein's consideration of the geometry of the visual field was instrumental to the development of his philosophy (and possibly what set him on the path to writing "Some Remarks on Logical Form"). One is that he asks: "How can the shape of a fleck in the visual field be described? Can coordinate geometry be done in the visual field [*Kann man im Gesichtsfeld Coordinatengeometrie treiben*]?" (2000, MS 105, 9), a second that he writes some pages later: "I am apparently thrown back against my will on arithmetic. The number is a means of representation" (19), and a third that he avers that the geometry of visual space is different from Euclidean geometry (45). While writing these remarks—all of which were drafted before the remarks in MS 105 that served as a basis for "Some Remarks on Logical Form"—Wittgenstein remained of the view that "[s]igns must have the multiplicity and qualities of the spaces" (55), from which it is no more than a short step to the conclusion that the mathematics of visual space is exceptional. Whence it directly follows that the logic detailed in the *Tractatus* is not the final word, signs referring to the phenomena of visual space failing to exhibit "the multiplicity and qualities" of Euclidean space.

On the present account of the shift in Wittgenstein's thinking, then, it was his reflections on the character of the visual field and mathematics (along perhaps with other considerations) that made the difference. When compiling the *Tractatus* in 1917/1918, he was committed to regarding the mathematical physicist's conception of representation as standing and falling with the logician's conception and he only came to repudiate this assumption in 1929. At this juncture he could retain his conception of colour as mathematically representable but not his conception of elementary propositions as number-free. He found he had to retract his earlier explanation of the attribution of more than one colour to a point as logically impossible (or, what amounts to the same thing, to accept that such attributions are logically impossible in a broader sense of logic). This in turn resulted in the idea of mathematical representation he had embraced very early on moving to centre stage and the idea of logical representation he had regarded as fundamental when writing the *Tractatus* fading into the background. In fact even as late as 1950 Wittgenstein was still wedded to the conception of a "mathematics" or "geometry" of colour and to explaining colour exclusion as a simple consequence of the logical structure of colour (1977, III-3 and III-86).[1]

---

1. *Acknowledgement*: I am indebted to William Demopoulos, W. D. Hart, Warren Ingber, Puqun Li and Marcos Silva for commenting on an earlier version of this paper and to Paul Forster for going through several drafts with a fine-tooth comb.

References

Black, Max 1964: *A Companion to Wittgenstein's 'Tractatus'*. Ithaca: Cornell University Press.

Dreben, Burton & Floyd, Juliet 1991: "How Not to Use a Word". *Synthese* 87, 23–49.

Engelmann, Mauro 2013: *Wittgenstein's Philosophical Development*. Basingstoke: Palgrave Macmillan.

Fogelin, Robert J. 1987: *Wittgenstein*. Second edition. London: Routledge.

Friedman, Michael 1999: *Reconsidering Logical Positivism*. Cambridge: Cambridge University Press.

Hacker, Peter M.S. 1986: *Insight and Illusion*. Revised edition. Oxford: Oxford University Press.

Hertz, Heinrich 1899: *The Principles of Mechanics*. New York: Cosimo Classics, 2007.

Hintikka, Merrill B. & Hintikka, Jaakko 1986: *Investigating Wittgenstein*. Oxford: Blackwell.

Landini, Gregory 2007: *Wittgenstein's Apprenticeship with Russell*. Cambridge: Cambridge University Press.

Lugg, Andrew 2003: "Wittgenstein's *Tractatus*: True Thoughts and Nonsensical Propositions". *Philosophical Investigations* 26, 332–347.

— 2013: "Wittgenstein's True Thoughts". *Nordic Wittgenstein Review* 2, 33–56.

— 2015: "Russell and Wittgenstein on Incongruent Counterparts and Incompatible Colours", *Russell: The Journal of Bertrand Russell Studies* 35, 43–58.

Pinsent, David H. 1990: *A Portrait of Wittgenstein as a Young Man*. Oxford: Blackwell.

Ramsey, Frank P. 1923: Review of "*Tractatus*". *Mind* 32, 465–478.

— 1990: *Philosophical Papers*. D.H. Mellor (ed.). Cambridge: Cambridge University Press.

Ricketts, Thomas 2013: "Logical Segmentation and Generality in Wittgenstein's *Tractatus*". In: Peter Sullivan & Michael Potter (eds.), *Wittgenstein's* Tractatus*: History and Interpretation*. Oxford: Oxford University Press, 125–142.

Russell, Bertrand 1903: *The Principles of Mathematics*. New York: Norton, 1964.

— 1927: *The Analysis of Matter*. London: Kegan Paul.

Waismann, Friedrich 1979: *Wittgenstein and the Vienna Circle*. Brian McGuinness (ed). Oxford: Blackwell.

White, Roger M. 2006: *Wittgenstein's* Tractatus Logico-Philosophicus. London: Continuum.

Wittgenstein, Ludwig 1922: *Tractatus Logico-philosophicus*. C.K. Ogden (trans.). London: Routledge and Kegan Paul, 1990.

Wittgenstein, Ludwig 1971: *Prototractatus*. London: Routledge & Kegan Paul.
— 1977: *Remarks on Colour*. Oxford: Blackwell.
— 1979: *Notebooks 1914–1916*. Second edition. Oxford: Blackwell.
— 1993: *Philosophical Occasions 1912–1951*. James Klagge and Alfred Nordmann (eds.). Indianapolis: Hackett.
— 1998: *Culture and Value*. Revised edition. Oxford: Blackwell.
— 2000: *Wittgenstein's Nachlass: The Bergen Electronic Edition*. Oxford: Oxford University Press.
— 2010: "The Ramsey Notes on Time and Mathematics". In: Nuno Venturinha (ed.), *Wittgenstein after his Nachlass*. Basingstoke: Palgrave Macmillan, 173–181.

DUMMETT'S CRITICISM OF THE CONTEXT PRINCIPLE

Philip A. EBERT
University of Stirling

Abstract
This paper discusses Michael Dummett's criticism of the Neo-Fregean conception of the context principle. I will present four arguments by Dummett that purport to show that the context principle is incompatible with platonism. I discuss and ultimately reject each argument. I will close this paper by identifying what I take to be a deep rooted tension in the Neo-Fregean project which might have motivated Dummett's opposition to the Neo-Fregean use of the context principle. I argue that this tension does give rise to a legitimate concern, yet it does not affect the Neo-Fregean conception of the context principle.

Keywords: Context Principle, Dummett, Neo-Fregeanism, singular terms, platonism

Introduction

This paper discusses Michael Dummett's criticism of the Neo-Fregean conception and application of the context principle. In the first section, I will outline what the Neo-Fregean interpretation—defended by Bob Hale and Crispin Wright—of the context principle amounts to. In the second section, I will distinguish two strands of criticism against this interpretation and, in the following section, discuss and subsequently reject the first type of criticism. In the fourth section, I will turn to the second strand of criticism and distinguish and discuss three different arguments put forth by Dummett. I show that none of these arguments are ultimately compelling and I will close this paper by identifying what I take to be a deep-rooted tension in the Neo-Fregean project which might have been the motivation for some of Dummett's concerns. I will suggest that although it is a legitimate tension, it is wrongly levelled against the Neo-Fregean conception of the context principle.

1. *The Neo-Fregean conception of the context principle*

The Neo-Fregeans interpret the context principle primarily as a thesis concerning what determines reference of singular terms.[1] Here, consider Frege's first characterisation of the context principle in the opening sections of the *Grundlagen*: "never to ask for the meaning [Bedeutung] of a word in isolation, but only in the context of a sentence" (Frege 1884, x). Crudely speaking the Neo-Fregean version of the context principle is gained by replacing "word" with "singular term" and by identifying Frege's use of "meaning" [Bedeutung] with reference. What is distinctive about the occurrence of singular terms in sentences, as opposed to those same terms in *isolation*, is that only in the context of the former can we determine their referential potential. So, reference of a singular term is established, provided there is a true sentence—of the appropriate (atomic) type—in which the singular term occurs.[2]

This idea has various consequences but first let me make out one point of affinity between Frege's context principle and the Neo-Fregean interpretation. As noted above, Frege claims that it is part of accepting the context principle that one should not ask for the meaning of a term in isolation. On the Neo-Fregean interpretation, this claim can be understood as preventing us from asking the additional question as to whether the singular term has a referent, even if all linguistic criteria for singular termhood are fulfilled *and* the truth of the statement is established. Doing otherwise, is to *isolate* questions of existence and thus to think that further investigations would yield an answer. On the Neo-Fregean reading this additional question is, at best, superfluous, if not incoherent.

So, the context principle—as understood by the Neo-Fregeans—says that if there is a singular term occurring in a true sentence (of the appropriate type) then the term refers. Now, since the term in question is a singular term, it will refer to an object (rather than some property). As such, this principle would not be of great interest unless the additional claim is made that the criteria of singular termhood can be established without direct appeal to the object presumed to be denoted by that term.[3] It is

---

1. See (Wright 1983, chapter 1 and section x), (Hale 1987) and (Hale and Wright 2002). For acomprehensive overview of the Neo-Fregean position, consult (MacBride 2003).

2. In this paper, I will not be concerned with what types of sentence do qualify as "appropriate" in the relevant sense. I will assume that an adequate characterisation and motivation for this category of sentences can be given and focus on more specific criticisms by Dummett.

3. For example, Field's nominalist position, e.g. (Field, 1989), is compatible with the con-

exactly this thought that is an important component in the Neo-Fregean interpretation of the context principle. The general idea is that there is a priority of linguistic questions or categories over ontological questions or categories: linguistic criteria suffice for recognising the referential potential of a term (whether it does refer obviously depends in addition on the truth and the appropriateness of the sentence it figures in). This type of "priority" of linguistic over ontological categories is further explicated in the following passage from Wright:

> By 'take priority' I mean simply this: questions of reference are not to have the independence that would make it possible to determine that a class of expressions have no genuine reference when, by the best syntactic criteria, these expressions function as singular terms in a range of statements [...] which we have every reason to suppose to be true. (Wright 1983, 25)

Hence, whether a term has referential potential (i.e. is to be regarded as a singular term which does refer if it figures in a true atomic sentence), can be established in virtue of certain syntactic criteria a term has to fulfil in order to be regarded as a singular term. This results in the idea that "the notion of an object is posterior in the order of explanation to that of a singular term" (Wright 1983, 24).[4] Crucially, this thesis which is, according to the Neo-Fregeans, tied to the context principle, puts the onus on its proponent to outline specific syntactic criteria independent of the notions of reference, or object, which would suffice to identify singular terms.

In the following, I will forgo any discussion of the syntactic criteria of singular termhood[5] and simply assume that such syntactic criteria can be made out and that number terms thereby feature as singular terms.

To summarise, the Neo-Fregean conception of the context principle comprises two key thoughts:

---

text principle in its minimalist form. It is just that for him the relevant mathematical sentences, despite involving singular terms, do not refer since the 'appropriate' sentences are, in fact, false.

4. Note that just before this passage, Wright identifies this thesis explicitly with the context principle. Similar views are later held by Wright. So, e.g. he claims one should "... treat syntactic categories,singular term and predicate, as primary in the order of explanation and the ontological categories object and concept/property as derivative. [...] But as far I can see [...] the general notion of an object remains: referent of a (possible) singular term." (Wright 1998b, 263).

5. See e.g. as proponents (Dummett 1981a, 54–80), (Hale 1979), (Hale 1995), (Hale 1996), (Wright1983, 10–12 and 53–64). For an overview of criticism, see (MacBride 2003) and more specific criticism (Williamson 1988) and (Wetzel 1990).

Minimal conception of the context principle
If there is a singular term occurring in an appropriate true sentence, then this term refers and there is an object which is the referent of this term.

Note that this claim is rather minimal; no priority of linguistic categories is mentioned and no constraint on the criteria for singular termhood is in place. In addition to the minimal conception a further claim is adopted, which is motivated by the priority of linguistic over ontological categories.

Syntactic Priority Thesis
Linguistic categories have priority over ontological ones and thus the criteria for singular termhood can be established without prerequisite appeal to the objects referred to by singular terms.

The Neo-Fregeans have argued that this version of the context principle is constitutive of a new form of platonism and that it plays an important role in resolving what is known as Benacerraf's dilemma.[6] Here, however, I won't be concerned with the issue of how the context principle can contribute to a satisfying answer to Benacerraf's challenge. Instead, the scope of this paper is restricted to a discussion of specific criticisms by Dummett against the Neo-Fregean usage of the context principle. That is, I will identify various arguments by Dummett that aim to show that the Neo-Fregean use of the context principle should be rejected or that it is incompatible with platonism.[7]

2. *Two types of criticism of the context principle*

The first type of criticism assumes that the context principle is correct but argues that if it were generally applicable, it would lead to problems since it either justifies false or contradictory statements or leads to problematic consequences in other areas of discourse. The following passage from Dummett fits nicely this first line of criticism:

---

6. This point is already made in (Wright 1983), yet it takes centre stage in (Hale and Wright 2002). Similar ideas are critically discussed in (Rosen 1993) and in (MacBride 2003). Benacerraf's dilemma is outlined in (Benacerraf 1973).

7. Concerns not discussed in this paper are, for example, the issue of impredicativity, see (Dummett 1991, 236) and (Dummett 1998), and the reductive character of abstraction principles, see (Rosen 1993) and (MacBride 2003).

> the contradiction was a catastrophe for Frege, not particularly because it exploded the notions of class and value range, but because it showed that justification [i.e. the context principle] to be unsound. It refuted the context principle, as Frege has used it. (Dummett 1991, 225)

In the next section I will discuss in detail one version of this criticism as put forward by Michael Dummett.

The second type of criticism aims to show that the context principle is incompatible with platonism. Crudely put: Dummett argues that the minimal reading of the context principle plus the syntactic priority thesis entail the claim that so-called pure abstract objects (such as numbers, sets, etc.) whose reference is established by the context principle, exist mind- or language-dependently. Thus, one cannot interpret the first two theses as justifying "real" reference to pure abstract objects. Rather, according to Dummett, we can only adopt some kind of "thin" reference, which will be insufficient for a platonist. In effect, Dummett aims to show that there is an irresolvable tension between adopting the context principle on the one hand, and resolving Benacerraf's challenge via the platonist route on the other. If Dummett is correct, the Neo-Fregeans are deeply misguided in thinking that the context principle can provide the basis for a platonist-conception of mathematics.

3. *The first type of criticism: The legitimating role of the context principle*

Dummett has claimed on various occasions that the context principle should be rejected because of the inconsistency of Basic Law V. Consider, e.g., the following two passages:

> What mattered philosophically, however, was not the definition in terms of classes, but the elimination of appeals to intuition, a condition for which was the justification of a general means of introducing abstract terms, as genuinely referring to non-actual objects, by determining the truth-conditions of sentences containing them. The contradiction was a catastrophe for Frege not particularly because it exploded the notion of class and value-range, but because it showed that justification to be unsound. It refuted the context principle, as Frege had used it. (Dummett 1991, 225)

> For Frege's method of introducing the abstraction operator—that is, of introducing value ranges—was, notoriously *not* in order. It rendered his system inconsistent; and that inconsistency forced him eventually to acknowledge

that his entire enterprise had failed. If the context principle, as stated by Wright, were sound, there could have been no inconsistency." (Dummett 1991, 88)

Let me briefly explain this last quotation: Frege's method of introducing the abstraction operator is the idea that abstraction principles introduce functions which, in the case of conceptual abstraction principles, are functions from properties to objects.[8] Frege's infamous Basic Law V is meant to introduce the value-range operator which maps coextensive properties (or: functions that map every object to the same value) to the same value-range. As is well-known Basic Law V is inconsistent.

The main thought in these two quoted passages seems to be that the fact that Basic Law V turned out to be inconsistent raises problems for the general application of the context principle. Disregarding for the moment possible differences in the context principle *as Frege used it* and *as stated by Wright*, Dummett's thought seems to be that the context principle *justifies* or *legitimates* abstraction principles in general. So, if on the basis of such justification an instance of such abstraction principles turns out to be inconsistent, then there is something wrong with its initial justification, namely the context principle. Hence, roughly we have the following short piece of reasoning: (1) The context principle legitimates the introduction of abstraction principles. (2) Some abstraction principles (e.g. Basic Law V) are inconsistent. Thus, (3) the context principle is defective as a legitimation for abstraction principles.

As it stands, this reasoning needs clarification and disambiguation. Let me outline two ways in which the idea of justification or legitimation can

---

8. The general form of an abstraction principle is:
$\forall\alpha\forall\beta(\xi(\alpha) = \xi(\beta) \leftrightarrow \alpha\approx\beta)$
where ξ is a term-forming operator applicable to expression of the type of α and β and $\approx$ is an equivalence relation on entities denoted by expressions of that type. If α and β stand for singular terms, the resulting (objectual) abstraction principle is first-order. If they stand for first-order predicates the resulting (conceptual) abstraction principle is second-order. An example of a first order or objectual abstraction principle is the *Direction Abstraction*:

The direction of line a is equal to direction of line b if and only if line a is parallel to line b. *Hume's Principle*, a principle which embedded in standard second-order logic yields the Peano axiom and so arithmetic, is a second-order or conceptual abstraction:

$\forall F \forall G((Nx:Fx = Nx:Gx) \leftrightarrow (F \approx G))$

where "Nx:Fx" stands for "the (cardinal) number of F's" and "$\approx$" expresses the equivalence relation of equinumerosity. Another example for conceptual abstraction principles is Frege's infamous Basic Law V, introducing the value-range operator (VR):

$\forall F \, \forall G(VR\!:\!F = VR\!:\!G \leftrightarrow \forall x(F(x) \leftrightarrow G(x)))$.

be understood and analyse why one might think that (1) is correct. On the first reading, the Neo-Fregeans use the context principle within the context of abstraction principles so that to be credited with an *understanding* of the new term—such as "the (cardinal) number of" in the case of Hume's Principle or "the value-range of" in the case of Basic Law V—it suffices to grasp the relevant abstraction principle. If the abstraction principle is successful, it fixes truth conditions of the identity statements in which the new expression figures by means of already understood terms that occur on the right-hand side of the abstraction principle. Now, if legitimation is understood in just this sense—i.e. what the context principle *legitimates* is that to be credited with an understanding of a new term grasping the relevant abstraction principle is sufficient—then this type of legitimation is not yet sufficient to provide a *guarantee* that abstraction principles, in general, are consistent. This reading of legitimation is concerned with the role of abstraction principles for a subject's understanding of a new term but not with whether the abstraction principle itself is consistent. Hence, this type of legitimation is not intended to effect the consistency of the underlying abstraction principle; nor is it prima facie necessary that the abstraction principle has to be consistent in order to provide an understanding of the new term involved. It might well be argued that even inconsistent abstraction principles can provide an understanding (albeit incomplete) of a new term.[9] If correct, the issue of consistency is independent of this type of legitimation and the argument is not compelling: it cannot be the aim of the intended legitimation to *guarantee* the consistency of an abstraction principle.

On the second reading we interpret the type of justification and legitimation the context principle offers as providing a guarantee that the new terms introduced in virtue of abstraction principles occur in true and thus consistent abstraction principles. This understanding of the context principle would make the occurrence of inconsistent abstraction principles very problematic indeed and so, the above reasoning would make a rather compelling point.[10]

---

9. Examples are Basic Law V, or the (unrestricted) T-schema for 'true'. To be sure, I'm not claiming that every inconsistent statement has a graspable content. It is enough—for current purposes—to point to some principles that despite their inconsistency provide some kind of understanding of the relevant term. This point is further developed in (Ebert, 2016). Also compare Frege's remark *Grundlagen*: "A concept is admissible even if its characteristic marks contain a contradiction." (Frege 1884, 105).

10. For instance, in a similar fashion to Dummett, Kit Fine argues against the context principle. In his book *Limits of Abstraction* he dedicates a chapter discussing the principle as

However, it is unclear why the context principle as previously outlined, i.e. the minimal reading and the syntactic priority thesis, should be regarded as comprising this strong sense of legitimation. The minimal reading of the context principle merely says that if there is a singular term occurring in a true sentence (of the appropriate type) then there is an object as the referent of that term, and as such it cannot provide a guarantee that the abstraction principle is true. The second component of the context principle—the syntactic priority thesis–cannot provide such a guarantee either. It merely claims that linguistic criteria have priority over ontological ones. Consequently, the context principle has no bearing on whether abstraction principles are true (and thus consistent) or not.[11]

To summarise, the context principle does not itself have any direct bearing on the truth of individual abstraction principles; the context principle only has an effect in that it guarantees reference of singular terms, provided the abstraction principle, in which the singular term occurs, is true. So, the the first kind of criticism levelled against the Neo-Fregean conception of the context principle fails to be compelling.[12]

4. *The second type of criticism*

In contrast to rejecting the application of the context principle altogether, Dummett also suggests that one could maintain the principle "but

---

used by the Neo-Fregeans. Therein, he supposes that "the 'context principle' can be regarded as an attempt to vindicate such contextual definitions." (Fine 2002, 55). (In this quotation 'contextual definitions' can be understood as involving abstraction principles.) Just as in the case of Dummett, it is unclear in Fine's writing to what extent the context principle is supposed to justify or vindicate such definitions. On various occasions, however, Fine seems to have a rather strong reading in mind. He regards the context principle as providing a justification that the abstraction principle so introduced is true. For a similar point against Fine, see (Cook and Ebert 2004, 798ff.).

11. This is not to say that the method that Wright uses in (Wright 1983) is without its problems: Wright's apparent unqualified assumption is that the introduction of an abstraction principle suffices, in all cases, to fix consistent truth-conditions for the relevant identity-statements. Surely this is objectionable, and it has since led to extensive discussions under the guise of so-called *Bad Company* objection: the challenge to provide appropriate conditions for *good* abstraction principles. My point here, however, is that this concern can be separated from the intelligibility of the context principle and so it cannot be used as a *reductio* on the context principle as outlined here.

12. This is, of course, not to say that Frege's original use of the context principle is unaffected by Dummett's criticism. I here focus only on a Neo-Fregean conception of the context principle and leave Frege scholarship for another occasion.

declare that it does not vindicate the procedure Wright has in mind." (Dummett 1991, 205). And here, what "Wright has in mind" is the thought that the context principle suffices to impose 'robust' or 'real' reference to abstract objects, such as numbers. In opposition to Wright, Dummett also believes that the context principle fails to guarantee a genuine reference relation to something existing independently. In the following, I will outline and discuss three separate lines of arguments in Dummett's writing that aim to undermine a 'realistic' or robust interpretation of the reference relation for abstract terms as introduced by the context principle.[13]

4.1 *The argument from disanalogy*

Dummett motivates a disanalogy between how we normally learn the use of singular terms purporting to refer to *concrete* objects and those that "seem" to refer to *abstract* objects.[14] The idea is roughly the following: In the concrete object case, we establish the reference of a term by the so-called *name-bearer prototype*, in which intuition—that is a perception of an object or a cognitive encounter with the object—plays a direct role in the identification and re-identification of the referent of the term. So, according to Dummett, to manifest an understanding of a newly introduced term purporting to refer to a concrete object is to exhibit the ability to identify the referent of this new expression—for example by understanding demonstrative phrases in which the new term occurs.[15]

In clear disanalogy, Dummett contends that this kind of manifestation does not seem to be possible for expressions purporting to refer to abstract objects. The role of the referent is minimised and it seems impossible— just because the object is abstract—to use the name-bearer prototype to establish a reference relation for the term. So, to manifest an understanding of this new term does not involve an appeal to the object purportedly referred to.

---

13. The relevant sections of Dummett are (Dummett 1981a, chapter 7 and 14), (Dummett 1981b, chapter 18, 19 and 20), and (Dummett 1991, chapters 15–18).

14. Dummett notes the disanalogy in (Dummett 1981a, 494) in the context of Goodman's nominalism. The use of the disanalogy as an argument can be found in (Dummett 1981a, 499) and most explicitly in (Dummett 1981a, 505). It reappears, using slightly different vocabulary, in (Dummett 1998, 384ff.).

15. Dummett is, of course, aware of Wittgensteinean consideration that mere ostensive definitions could not establish this relationship. However, Wittgensteinean worries will be left untouched in my discussion.

Based on this disanalogy, Dummett concludes that abstract terms do not have genuine reference (i.e. reference to something externally existing). The inference to this conclusion is supported by the claim that intuition has to play a certain role in the *identification* of the referent for there to be a genuine reference relation to something external; and if it does not, the term has no genuine referential relation to something external. Differently put, for the case of abstract terms the role of reference is *semantically idle* as the referent does not play a role in determining the truth-value of statements in which it figures, i.e. no intuition is involved in determining the truth-value of statements involving the new term. Therefore, no real reference can be assumed for abstract terms. In contrast, the role of reference in the case of terms standing for concrete objects is *semantically operative* in that intuition is essential in manifesting an understanding of the term. A version of this argument can be found in the following passage by Dummett:

> I proposed for a notion of reference for singular terms to be robust enough to support a realistic interpretation [...] that their reference should be semantically operative. Whether a notion of reference for terms of a given range is semantically operative or semantically idle depends on the sense we attach to the sentence containing a term of that range. In grasping its sense, we have a conception of the way in which its truth-value is determined. If the determination of the truth-value of any such sentence goes *through the identification of the referent of the term*, the notion of reference, as applied to it, is *semantically operative*; if it does not that notion, even though legitimate, is *semantically idle*. (Dummett 1998, 385) my italics, see also (Dummett 1991, 239)

And in a further (and earlier) passage Dummett again makes a similar point:

> But precisely the point at which the analogy fails is in the use of the realist picture: the recognition of the truth of a numerical equation cannot be described as the identification of an object external to us as the referent of a term, precisely because there is no sense in which it requires us to discern numbers as constituents of the external world. (Dummett 1981a, 505)

The conclusion Dummett aims to draw from this is not that no reference to abstract objects can be assumed, which would be to support a form of nominalism that Dummett previously rejected. Instead, we merely cannot assume robust reference—reference to an independently existing entity—in the case of terms introduced in virtue of contextual definition (or abstraction principles).

Consequently, Dummett introduces a less substantial "thin" notion of reference on the grounds that there is a clear disanalogy between prototype cases of how reference functions in concrete cases and cases where abstract objects are involved. Compare the following quotation from Dummett concerning the reference of new terms introduced in virtue of contextual definitions:

> In such a case [of contextual definition], no view stronger than an intermediate one could be taken of a claim that a reference had thereby been conferred upon them [i.e. the new terms]; the reference so conferred would be reference only in the thin sense […], since the notion would play no role in the semantic account of how the truth-values of sentences containing the terms are determined. (Dummett 1991, 236)[16]

As it stands, I believe that Dummett's argument from disanalogy can be challenged on at least three grounds:

1. Grant the disanalogy but show that something else can be regarded as fulfilling the role of the name-bearer prototype in the abstract case, which thereby guarantees a real reference relation for abstract terms.
2. Challenge Dummett's crucial transition from the claim that intuition is not necessary for manifesting our understanding in the case of abstract singular terms to the claim that therefore they do not refer realistically.
3. Challenge the coherence of Dummett's own proposal concerning "thin" reference.

The first line of response has been pursued by Wright[17], but I will leave a detailed discussion of this strategy aside. I believe that this discussion ends in a stand-off between Dummett and Wright and as such won't be sufficient to undermine Dummett's argument. Instead, I will focus on what I think is wrong with Dummett's argument by focusing on the second strategy and then raise some doubts about the coherence of his position by pursuing the third strategy.

---

16. See also the following passage: "The proponent of the intermediate view of terms introduced by contextual definition—the view for which I have here argued—maintains that the thin notion of reference will not bear the weight of a realistic interpretation of those terms;" (Dummett 1991, 198)
17. Compare here (Wright 1983, section x).

4.1.1 *First rejoinder: Dummett's illicit inference*

In order for Dummett's argument from disanalogy to have force he requires a strong assumption, which consists in moving from the role an object plays in our *understanding* of the term referring to it, to conclusions about its *ontological* status. More precisely, Dummett's argument starts out with the intuitive claim that in the case of concrete objects where we do have real reference, intuition plays a crucial role in manifesting our understanding and thereby settling the reference of a term. In the case of abstract terms, intuition does not play any such role in our understanding of the term, a point that again is intuitive. But from this, Dummett draws the ontological conclusion that the object referred to does not exist externally, i.e. mind-independently. However, what is it that underwrites such a transition? I think that the transition cannot be upheld in general. In order to highlight my worries consider the following two questions:[18]

1. Do we need intuition to justify or manifest that we understand new terms figuring in certain sentences (say sentence S)?
2. Do the objects referred to by the new terms involved in the sentence S exist mind-independently?

If I understand Dummett correctly, he seems to be committed to answering the second question with "no" provided that he returns a negative answer to the first. But I find it hard to detect a compelling reason to think this being correct. Consider, for example, sentences in modern theoretical physics involving mainly theoretical terms (such as "strings", "neutrinos", etc.) or other theoretical terms such as "the equator", "the north pole". In this case, manifesting our understanding of such terms does not seem to involve any intuition in the sense of having a perception of the object or a cognitive encounter with it. And yet the lack of this type of encounter does not seem to have any bearing on the ontological status of the objects involved. As a result, I regard the general application of this transition as questionable at best; and so the onus is on Dummett to provide some reasons why there is such a strong link between these two issues.

However, there may be a weaker reading of the argument, namely, that based on the disanalogy, the *default reason* to think that abstract terms refer realistically is lacking. Hence, unless there is independent reason to think

---

18. The distinction I am about to make is similar to one made by (Hale 1987, 165ff.).

otherwise—and arguably in the physics case there is—we should conclude that such terms do not genuinely refer to mind-independent objects.[19]

Even granting this much, I think that, dialectically, some reason for making the transition from understanding a term to the ontological status of the object referred to is required. Otherwise it is unclear why the name-prototype is a default reason for mind-independent existence. Furthermore, the platonist might well be credited with having independent reasons for thinking that numbers and sets exist mind-independently. So, for example the belief that mathematical truths are necessary could give rise to the belief that the objects referred to are mind-independent. Either way, Dummett's argument seems to involve an unmotivated assumption and even the more favourable version of the argument can be challenged.

Thus, let me now turn to the conclusion of Dummett's *argument from disanalogy* and challenge the coherency of his own conception of "thin" reference.

4.1.2 *Second rejoinder: Some scruples about "thin" reference*

Dummett claims that there is a type of reference—"thin" reference—which is a genuine reference relation, even though it lacks the realistic underpinnings of robust reference. Dummett says very little about the characteristics of this notion of reference. The aim of this section is to suggest different ways of interpreting "thin" reference and to raise doubts as to whether Dummett is entitled to claim that "thin" reference is a genuine reference relation.

First, let us investigate why Dummett thinks he is entitled—within his framework—to assume that abstract terms actually do refer, but merely "thinly". As noted, Dummett regards robust reference as a relation that only holds if it is embedded in intuition and in this way the term becomes semantically operative. But then, if there is no intuition and nothing else in which the reference relation is embedded, on what grounds can Dummett maintain that when the terms are not semantically operative (i.e. they are semantically idle), there still is a genuine, yet only "thin" reference relation? Why isn't it the case that these are non-referring terms?

To highlight this problem, let me put forth the following dilemma for the Dummettian position: Either he offers an alternative to intuition which

---

19. I knowingly pass over agnosticism as an alternative conclusion. It seems to me that, at best, Dummett's arguments only give rise to agnosticism.

underwrites the reference relation in the case of abstract terms; but then it could be argued—along the first line of response which I did not discuss in any detail—that these grounds suffice to ensure "real" reference and not merely "thin" reference. Or, alternatively, Dummett does not provide an alternative to intuition, which would then open up the option to reject any type of reference relation—even "thin" reference.

Here, I will leave this dilemma as an open challenge, and turn to the issue of disambiguating various interpretations of Dummett's notion of "thin" reference. The aim is to clarify what exactly it is that is supposedly "thin" about this sort of reference. Two possible interpretations can be considered.

1. That the relation of reference is somehow itself "thin" or deflated.
2. The referent, i.e. the object referred to, is "thin" in some sense.

Concerning the first interpretation the question is what it is for the relation itself to be "thin". I will suggest three ways this could be made sense of. One possible interpretation is that "thin" reference for abstract terms means that the relation holds at best indeterminately.[20] However, usually the idea of indeterminate reference is not regarded as in any way less "substantial" than the normal one. It is normally regarded as still picking out (albeit indeterminately) independently existing objects. So, it seems that Dummett's conception of "thin" reference has to be understood differently.

The second suggestion results from unpacking a quote from Dummett:

> The context principle, as understood in the *Grundlagen*, therefore admits only a thin notion of reference, that notion according to which '"The direction of a" refers to something' is indisputably true, because it reduces to 'The line a has a direction', and '"The direction of a" refers to the direction of a', [is] trivially true, because it reduces to 'The direction of a is the direction of a'. The context principle of the *Grundlagen* is thus strictly analogous to the redundancy theory of truth according to which '"Cleanliness is next to godliness" is true' reduces to 'Cleanliness is next to godliness.' (Dummett 1991, 195)

Now, this *disquotational* conception of "thin" reference can be combined with other theses that Dummett held, namely: (i) we have to have the resources to distinguish referring and non-referring terms in the object-

---

20. See for example (Fine 1975) where he provides a formal framework, i.e. supervaluationist semantics for indeterminate reference.

language; (ii) the tolerant reductionist view that "our grasp of the thought expressed by a sentence containing the term is mediated by our knowledge (possibly only implicit) of how to arrive at an equivalent sentence not containing that term." (Dummett 1991, 193) If we combine these ideas, then we arrive at the conclusion that a reductionist can tolerate someone saying—in the object language—that certain entities (such as directions) exist, even though our meta-linguistic account of them uses other entities (lines). Thus, there is, strictly speaking, no commitment to directions and in that sense we merely have a "thin" reference relation.

The main difficulty with this interpretation, however, is that it seems highly questionable whether "thin" reference so understood is not just a denial of a genuine reference *relation* altogether. After all, it reduces merely to a disquotation-device and we are left wondering whether there is a relation that holds between the term "direction" and the object (direction). It seems to me that this interpretation comes very close to reading "thin" reference as involving no reference at all: reference is here a mere *façon de parler*.[21]

A similar concern applies to the third suggestion, which can be extracted from earlier writings of Dummett. In his *Frege: Philosophy of Language* he distinguished two types of reference relations, normal or *name-bearer prototype* reference and reference as *semantic role*. Might the latter be of help interpreting his later notion of "thin" reference—this despite the fact that Dummett never explicitly identified them?[22] The difference between the two notions is that the normal (or prototype) reference is regarded as a relation between a term and something extra-linguistic, whereas reference as semantic role is defined by the contribution the expression makes to the determination of the truth-value of sentences in which it occurs.[23] We are once again left with a conception of reference where there is no genuine reference *relation*. In fact, Dummett's notion of reference as semantic role seems very close to the notion of a Fregean sense.[24]

---

21. An allusion to the following passage in Dummett: "[Frege's] 'context' doctrine of meaning may be accepted as an explanation and defence of the use of abstract terms, but reference may be ascribed to them only as a *façon de parler*." (Dummett 1981a, 508)

22. Dummett's discussion of reference as semantic role took place 20 years earlier in (Dummett 1981a, 204–45). Hale (1987) and Wright (1983) often use the idea of 'reference as semantic role' as an interpretation of "thin" reference.

23. See for example (Dummett 1981a, 210f).

24. To strengthen the exegetical suggestion that Dummett's reference as semantic role is similar to the notion of Fregean sense requires a more detailed investigation. I will, however, postpone further discussion of this point to another occasion.

A more promising interpretation might be to think of the notion of "thin" as applying to the referent and not to the reference relation. Consequently, to invoke the idea of "thin" reference is another way to say that abstract terms refer, but the objects referred to are somehow "thin". If that is the right way of looking at Dummett's notion of "thin" reference, and if, as I argued, the argument from disanalogy fails, then an alternative argument is needed to establish the *ontological* claim that abstract terms refer to mere "thin" objects. In the next section, I discuss such an argument.[25]

4.2 *Pure abstract objects and the argument from analyticity*

Dummett's second argument is based on a distinction about the nature of objects. He distinguishes abstract objects in general from what he calls *pure* abstract objects. Examples of the former type are objects to which terms refer that have been introduced contextually by means of abstraction principles involving concrete objects on their right-hand side, as in the case of directions.[26] Other examples that are mentioned in the literature involve terms that are introduced by a demonstrative combined with a so-called functional expression.[27] Pure abstract objects, in contrast, are characterised as those "whose existence *may be recognised* independently of any concrete object, and therefore independently of any observation of the world." (Dummett 1981a, 504, my italics.) And for Dummett these are objects to which terms refer that are introduced in virtue of second-order abstraction principles, where one does not abstract on objects but on concepts, as is the case in Hume's Principle.[28] On another occasion, Dummett characterises pure abstract objects as those "whose existence is analytic."(Dummett 1981a, 505)[29]

---

25. Dummett's notion of "thin" reference has been discussed in the literature. For example, (Hale 1994), (Wright 1998a) and (Wright 1995). The discussion below, however, is independent of the previous debate.

26. See footnote 8 for further details on the direction abstraction principle. However, note that not all objectual abstraction principles will give rise to abstract objects. Some might give rise to pure abstract objects, see e.g. Hale's difference-pairs abstraction in (Hale 2000).

27. An example of a functional expression is the notion "shape", which can be introduced with the statement "the shape of this figure" accompanied with an appropriate pointing gesture. See Dummett on "functional" expressions in (Dummett 1981a, 176-9). To stress, the above examples for abstract objects are just that, examples, and not intended as providing necessary and sufficient conditions. The exact conditions need not concern us here.

28. Again see footnote 8 for further details on Hume's Principle.

29. I assume what Dummett here means is that an existential statement involving such objects is an analytic truth. See also below.

Let us grant Dummett the distinction between abstract and pure abstract objects. What he aims to show is that pure abstract objects cannot be "constituents of an external reality". One argument in which the notion of a pure abstract object seems to play a role is in the following quotation:

> …, but for, say, shapes of physical bodies the sequences of concrete objects, the use of these terms is still clearly related to processes of observation of the external world and identification of constituents of it. For that reason, therefore, it is still possible to apply to such terms the notion of reference, construed realistically as a relation to something external; although, indeed, the further we travel along the scale, the more stretched becomes the analogy with the prototypical case. It is only when we reach terms for pure abstract objects, however, that the thread snaps completely, and we are concerned with the use of terms which have no external reference at all. (Dummett 1981a, 510)

There are at least two readings of this remark. The first is one in which the "snapping of the thread" is due to the fact that the prototypical case of reference does not apply and so we are back at the earlier argument from disanalogy. The second reading, however, assigns the notion of a pure abstract object a distinct role in arriving at the conclusion that pure abstract singular terms do not have external reference. In a previous section, Dummett mentions the following additional consideration about pure abstract objects which might support this reading:

> But the picture does seem to require that what may be called a 'constituent of reality' is something which can be encountered; and, if the existence of something is an analytic truth, a recognition of its existence can hardly be held to constitute an encounter." (Dummett 1981a, 503)

Combining this thought with the first quotation, we can reconstruct the following *argument from analyticity*:

PREMISE 1 In order for a term to have external reference, minimally, the object it purports to refer to has to be a 'constituent of reality'.
PREMISE 2 For an object to be a constituent of reality it has to be encounterable in some sense.
PREMISE 3 Objects whose existential statement is an analytic truth are not encounterable in any relevant sense.[30]

---

30. I simplified this point. Dummett talks about "a recognition of its existence" not involving an encounter; but I assume that this entails, in general, that recognizing their existence cannot involve an encounter.

CONCLUSION "The thread snaps": pure abstract terms do not have reference to an external object.

Now, since the argument is aimed at a platonist, we need to be careful in interpreting load-bearing notions involved such as "constituent of reality" and "encounterable". It would be question-begging to take "constituent of reality" in premise 1 and 2 to require that such a constituent has to be spatio-temporally located. Furthermore, Dummett's notion of "encounterable" cannot just be understood to mean "perceivable by a subject" or "capable of causal interaction". Consider, for example, premise 3 and assume with Dummett that numbers are objects whose existence is analytic. That is, according to Dummett, we recognise their existence without encountering them. Certainly, if "encounterable" is here understood as "capable of causal interaction" then premise 3 could well be regarded as true (even by the platonist), yet premise 2 will beg the question. So, in order to run the argument without begging the question, what is needed is an interpretation of the notions "constituent of reality" and "encounterable" which avoids these problems. In addition, we need an understanding of these notions which allows abstract objects but not pure abstract objects to be encounterable or to be constituents of reality. This latter constraint is needed in order to respect Dummett's rejection of nominalism. I find it hard to offer any suitable understanding of these notions which respects the above constraints. Given this, I will leave it as an open challenge for the Dummettian to come up with a suitable interpretation and thus (tentatively) conclude that the argument from analyticity fails to be compelling at this stage.

4.3 *The argument from conceptualisation*

A further argument, that I will label the argument from conceptualisation, can be found in Dummett's work.[31] The following quotation provides the gist of the argument:

> When we apply the conceptual apparatus with which language supplies us to reality, this results in the discernment of a variety of objects, concrete and abstract: but the apparatus is such that certain objects will be recognised however the reality is constituted to which we apply it; these are pure abstract objects, like the natural numbers, whose existence is analytic. This is incom-

---

31. Interestingly, it disappears in his later writings although the argument plays an important role in the chapter entitled Abstract Objects in (Dummett 1981a).

prehensible if we think of the world as composed of objects, as coming to us already segmented into objects: in that case, how could there be a whole plurality of eternally existing, uncreated objects? But, once we realise that our apprehension of reality as decomposable into discrete objects is the product of our application to an unarticulated reality of the conceptual apparatus embodied in our language [1], it should not be particularly surprising that certain objects should result from this operation no matter what the reality is like [2] to which it is applied.

Perhaps not: yet for that reason it appears impossible to regard the pure abstract objects as constituent of an external reality [3]." (Dummett 1981a, 504f.)

Again, I will try to transform this reasoning into a more perspicuous three step argument, followed by a brief discussion of Hale's reply to the argument and my own evaluation of the various points raised.

The first premise [1] is Dummett's claim about how the structure of language shapes our apprehension of reality. It is what I call the *Objects qua Conceptualisation Thesis (OCT)*:

> PREMISE 1 (OCT) The apprehension of reality as having distinct objects is dependent upon the usage of the conceptual apparatus supplied by language.[32]

This premise is somewhat vague. It is not clear what exactly this dependence amounts to. Furthermore, note that what is claimed is not that the *existence* of objects is somehow dependent upon our language—a precariously strong claim—but rather that our *apprehension* of reality as having objects depends upon our conceptual scheme. Also, Dummett thinks this premise follows directly from the adoption of the context principle (more on this below).

The second point [2] Dummett makes is a restriction to *pure abstract objects*.

> PREMISE 2 Certain objects may "result" from the operation of conceptualisation alone, i.e. no matter what reality is like.

---

32. Similar expressions of the same thought are "what objects we recognise the world as containing depends on the structure of our language" (Dummett 1981a, 503), "it is we who, by the use of language, ... impose structure on it."(Dummett 1981a, 504) and "it is only because we employ a language ... that we learn to slice the world up, conceptually, into discrete objects." (Dummett 1981a, 407)

Again, this premise needs some sharpening. I shall abandon Dummett's modal talk and assume that his point in premise 2 is that, in fact, certain objects, such as pure abstract objects, result solely from operations of conceptualisation. Interestingly, this premise seems not to concern our apprehension of such objects as resulting from conceptualisation but suggests that it is the objects themselves that result from these operations of conceptualisation.

Lastly, putting the two premisses together, Dummett arrives at the conclusion:

> CONCLUSION Pure abstract objects are not constituents of an external reality.

There is much to say about the argument. On first sight, it seems as if various steps are missing in order to arrive at the conclusion. One thought might be that there is something similar in play as in the previous *argument from analyticity*: Because certain objects result from conceptualisation and their existence is "analytic", it follows that they cannot be constituents of an external reality. However, there is another interpretation of Dummett's argument which is independent of the above *argument from analyticity* and which has been discussed by Hale.

Hale's strategy is to show that Dummett relies on an implicit assumption for the argument to go through. By highlighting it, he offers a new interpretation of the structure of Dummett's argument. To reveal this assumption, he questions what exactly restricts the denial of an external reality to pure abstract objects and why does it not apply to impure abstracts or even concrete objects. The reply on behalf of Dummett is stressing premise 2, namely that pure abstract objects result solely on the basis of our conceptual apparatus and *no matter what the reality to which we apply it is like*. However, Hale questions why this should constitute a relevant difference and concludes that there is a relevant difference only if the following additional claim is adopted. Hale writes:

> It would be so [i.e. that there would be a relevant difference], if it were assumed that, for objects of some kind to be constituents of an external reality, their existence must be a contingent matter—that is, it must depend upon just how the world is, as a matter of fact, in respects to which it could have been otherwise. (Hale 1987, 157)

So, premise 2 makes a relevant difference only if the additional thesis, call it *Mind-independent Existence is Contingent (MEC)*, is assumed:

> For objects to exist externally, i.e. mind-independently, their existence must be a contingent matter, i.e. it is dependent on how the world is and thus could have been otherwise." (Hale 1987, 157)

Given this the argument seems in better shape. Yet, Hale argues that (MEC) is implausible because it relies in turn on another, even more problematic assumption. He writes:

> But why make this assumption [MEC]? Well, that would, it seems, be a fair assumption, if, but only if, it were the case that all necessity is of our making—the inevitable, but metaphysically innocuous byproduct, as it were, of our efforts of conceptualisation. In short, if this diagnosis of the underpinnings of Dummett's argument is correct, its capacity to undermine platonism depends, after all, upon the tenability of some sort of conventionalist reduction of necessity. (Hale 1987, 157)

Hale's interpretation is revealing but some further questions remain. First and foremost, what role exactly does OCT (premise 1) play in the original argument? The following reconstruction based on Hale's interpretation seems valid as a self-contained argument:

PREMISE 1* MEC For objects to exist externally, i.e. mind-independently, their existence must be a contingent matter.
PREMISE 2* Certain objects, such as pure abstract objects "result" from the operation of conceptualisation alone, i.e. no matter what the reality is like and thus exist necessarily.
CONCLUSION Pure abstract objects do not exist externally and so do not exist mind-independently.

So, MEC, plus the thought that pure abstract objects exist necessarily, are already sufficient for the conclusion and thus premise 1—i.e. OCT—is irrelevant.

Second, it is not clear that adopting a conventionalist view on necessity is necessary and sufficient for MEC. It seems possible to adopt MEC and reject the conventional character of necessity and, conversely, it seems equally possible to adopt a conventionalist account of necessity and reject MEC. Only if the additional thesis is adopted that the metaphysical status of a kind of object (as being mind-dependent or mind-independent) just is a question about the metaphysical status of truths about these objects, can a link be established between the two claims. It is noteworthy that Hale explicitly adopts this additional thesis throughout his discussion. He writes, "what is required for those objects to be 'external' or constituents of a mind-independent reality [...] is best seen as, at bottom, a question about the (metaphysical) status of the truths of the corresponding sort—viz. do these truths hold independently of us/of our thought and talk?" (Hale 1987, 165). Here, I do not want to deny this link but rather point out that there is logical space for alternative views.

More importantly, let me offer some evaluation of Dummett's argument. First, if it relies on MEC, then I think it should be rejected. So, for example, according to MEC, it is a necessary condition for an object to exist mind-independently that its existence is a contingent matter. So, to take the example of God: Assume that if God were to exist, he would exist necessarily, but then, according to MEC, he would have to exist mind-dependently. Also on this conception, pure sets, i.e. sets without individuals in the transitive closure of the membership relation, would exist mind-dependently. Yet, it remains open whether objects such as impure sets, such as the singleton of some contingent object, which, at least prima facie is a contingently existing abstract object, exists also mind-independently. Thus, MEC is highly questionable.

The following suggestion might help to provide some motivation for an alternative interpretation of Dummett's reasoning. It may be derived from the "artefact of the model" metaphor as defended by Stewart Shapiro:

> Typically, some features of a given mathematical model correspond to features of reality that is being modelled and some do not. The latter are called artefacts of the model, and let us call the former 'representors'. In a point-mass model of a physical system, the co-ordinate system, the units of measure and the notation for numbers are artefacts of the model. They do not correspond to anything in real physical systems. The metric and various relationships between forces and distances, like the inverse-square principle, are representors, not artefacts. Notice that, in a given case, it may not be clear what is representor and what is artefact and perhaps the boundary is not sharp." (Shapiro 1998, 139).

We could apply this idea to Dummett's writing in the following way: Namely, certain objects, such as pure abstract objects, that come about "no matter what reality is like" are in this respect mere "artefacts of our conceptualisation". They come about through conceptualizing and are artefacts and not representors. As a result they cannot be regarded as existing genuinely mind-independently. Maybe it is a consideration like this that underlies Dummett's *argument from conceptualisation*.

However, even if that is so, Dummett has not yet explained why, adopting this talk of artefacts in the case of pure abstract objects, these kinds of objects would qualify as genuine artefacts. More precisely, he has to explain away the alternative account of why pure abstract objects always exist in any conceptualisation: It is just because objects such as pure abstract objects do exist necessarily and mind-independently That is, a correct and complete conceptualisation of the world will always have to involve such objects. So, on this platonist view, the order of determination is reversed and it is not because of our conceptualisation that certain objects exist or result (that is the artefact view); rather, it is because certain objects exist necessarily and mind-independently that we end up always conceptualising these object (provided it is a correct and complete conceptualisation).

So, to conclude, I believe that Dummett's argument from conceptualisation also fails to move his opponent. This is because, if Hale's interpretation is correct and Dummett's argument relies on MEC, then he needs to provide a genuine motivation for adopting MEC, as well as explain away the various counterintuitive consequences. Alternatively, we have suggested that Dummett's own conception could be explained by taking pure abstract objects as a kind of artefact. This interpretation of the argument, however, makes apparent that there is an alternative explanation of the phenomenon of pure abstract objects, one that is both well motivated and clearly accepted by his opponent. Hence, from this perspective of evaluation, Dummett's consideration is not convincing either. Lastly, it is worth noting that if the argument relies on a conventional account of necessity, then this assumption is problematic not only because it seems to lead to MEC but also because of various convincing arguments against such an account of necessity, which I cannot cover here.[33]

One remaining question is whether there is a further, alternative interpretation that makes use of Dummett's initial premise 1. In the following section, I will suggest a reading which should not be understood as a direct argument against pure abstract singular terms and their referential ability, but it is meant to exhibit a potential tension. As Dummett writes:"There is, undisputably, a considerable tension between Frege's realism and the doctrine of meaning only in context [i.e. the context principle]: the question is whether it is a head-on collision."(Dummett 1981a, 499).

---

33. See especially (Quine 1960) and (Quine 1935). Dummett himself has criticised a certain form of conventionalism in (Dummett 1959).

5. *Analysing Dummett's tension*

The aim is to try to develop a prima facie tension within the Neo-Fregean view between the adoption of the context principle on the one hand and platonism on the other. It can be developed by reconsidering premise 1, as Dummett writes:

> The apprehension of reality as having distinct objects is dependent upon the usage of the conceptual apparatus" and thus that "what objects we recognise the world as containing depends on the structure of our language" (Dummett 1981a, 503).

According to Dummett, this claim follows from the context principle: a language-dependent apprehension of objects flows from the syntactic priority component of the context principle. Consequently, one can arrive at premise 1 of Dummett's argument because it is through singular terms and linguistic categories in general that we explain and grasp things as objects—our apprehension of objects depends (in parts) on our linguistic framework.

Why might this idea be regarded as being in tension with platonism, i.e. the thought that pure abstract objects exist mind-independently?[34] One might argue that if certain abstract or pure abstract objects do exist mind-independently, any reference to these objects is a relation to something whose existence and character is viewed as independent of our modes of conceiving of them and our modes of talking about them. This, so one might think, is in tension with premise 1 that our apprehension of objects crucially depends on our linguistic framework.

Maybe—but only maybe—it is this alleged basic tension that Dummett discerns within the Neo-Fregean programme. He thinks that such a tension can be avoided for concrete objects, but that it is problematic in the case of pure abstract objects. In the following, I suggest that this worry can be avoided, if it is meant to be a problem for the context principle and platonism. I will then consider whether a similar tension can be discerned within the Neo-Fregean project, if it is re-located in their conception of abstraction principles.

There is an important constraint on whether, according to the Neo-Fregeans, we can apprehend or grasp objects through singular terms as warranted by the context principle: Namely, singular terms have to figure in *true* sentences. And, it is perfectly compatible with the context principle that our apprehension of reality is, in certain circumstances, incorrect. This

---

34. This is a somewhat crude characterisation of platonism which, however, suffices for our purposes here. For a more detailed discussion of different forms of platonism, see (Linnebo 2011).

can happen, if, to speak crudely, the world does not co-operate and the sentences in virtue of which "apprehension" apparently takes place actually turn out to be false, despite initially good reasons for thinking otherwise. Consequently, we can only legitimately say that there is an object as referent of an abstract singular term if we have sufficient reasons to hold such sentences true – and even then such reasons may be considered defeasible. Furthermore, if the notion of truth for the relevant sentences is sufficiently robust, then there is no tension between our apprehension of the objects being language-dependent on the one hand, and the mind-independent existence of these objects on the other. Hence, there does not have to be a 'head-on collision'.

Nevertheless, and this might be Dummett's underlying worry, the question is whether the Neo-Fregeans are entitled to assume that abstraction principles do involve a notion of truth robust enough for their purpose. That is, the question is whether the idea of *stipulating* the truth of an abstraction principle—such that they are *true by fiat*—presupposes a conventional element which cannot involve a notion of truth *robust* enough. So, one might think that if we arrive at an apprehension of objects purely in virtue of stipulations, then these objects cannot also be regarded as mind-independent. This might be a way to account for a prima facie tension for the Neo-Fregean approach and platonism.

However, if that is what Dummett had in mind, then the tension is wrongly located: It is an issue for a defender of abstraction principles—or implicit definitions in general—involving the idea of stipulation; not for a defender of the context principle—the minimal conception and the syntactic priority thesis. It is consistent to adopt both the context principle and platonism yet reject the idea that stipulation is a legitimate method for introducing (robustly) true sentences. Hence, if there is such a tension it has to be resolved by the Neo-Fregeans within a theory of implicit definitions and abstraction principles.[35]

6. *Conclusions*

In this paper, I hope to have clarified what the content of the Neo-Fregean conception of the context principle is and I have identified four different arguments in Dummett's writing against it. I have argued that none of

---

35. For further discussion on the Neo-Fregen conception of implicit definitions and stipulation, see (Hale and Wright 2000), (Wright 2016), and (Ebert 2016).

these arguments are compelling. This is, of course, not to deny that there are other issues raised and also argued for by Dummett (such as impredicativity, or the Caesar problem) that may undermine the viability of the Neo-Fregean programme. Thus, in this respect my results are modest: I merely claim to have shown that the context principle—in the version outlined here and as used in the Neo-Fregean programme—is still a viable and compelling principle despite Dummett's arguments. Moreover, I hope to have identified a basic worry that might have been Dummett's motivation for his opposition to the context principle. However, I believe that this concern should not be regarded as motivating a rejection of the context principle as such; rather, it is a worry that is best levelled against the possibility of stipulating the (robust) truth of certain sentences (such as abstraction principles or implicit definitions in general)—an idea that is also at the heart of the Neo-Fregean project.[36]

References

Benacerraf, Paul 1973: "Mathematical Truth". *Journal of Philosophy* 70, 661–80. Reprinted in: Benacerraf & Putnam, 1983.

Benacerraf, Paul & Putnam, Hillary 1983: *Philosophy of Mathematics*. Second edition. Cambridge: Cambridge University Press.

Cook, Roy T & Ebert, Philip A. 2004: "Discussion Note: Kit Fine, Limits of Abstraction". *British Journal for the Philosophy of Science* 55, 791–800.

Dummett, Michael 1959: "Wittgenstein's Philosophy of Mathematics". *The Philosophical Review* 68(3), 324–48. Reprinted in: Dummett, 1978.

— 1978: *Truth and other Enigmas*. Cambridge, Mass: Harvard Press.

— 1981a: *Frege: Philosophy of Language*. Second edition Cambridge, Mass: Harvard Press.

— 1981b: *The Interpretation of Frege's Philosophy*. Cambridge, Mass: Harvard Press.

— 1991: *Frege: Philosophy of Mathematics*. Cambridge, Mass: Harvard Press.

— 1998: "Neo-Fregeans: In Bad Company". In: Matthias Schirn (ed),*Philosophy of Mathematics Today*. Oxford: Oxford University Press, 369–87.

---

36. I would like to thank Fraser MacBride, Walter Pedriali, Marcus Rossberg, Crispin Wright, and two anonymous referees for comments on earlier versions. Also, I would like to thank the audiences at Bristol, St Andrews, and Stirling for comments that have helped to improve the paper. This work was supported by a grant from the UK Arts and Humanities Research Council: AH/J00233X/1.

Ebert, Philip A. 2016. "A Framework for Implicit Definitions". In Philip Ebert & Marcus Rossberg (eds), *Abstractionism*. Oxford: Oxford University Press.

Field, Hartry. 1989: *Science without Numbers*. Oxford: Blackwell Publisher.

Fine, Kit 1975: "Vagueness, Truth and Logic". *Synthese* 30, 265–300. Reprinted in: Keefe & Smith, 1997.

— 2002: *Limits of Abstraction*. Oxford: Oxford University Press.

Frege, Gottlob 1884: *Die Grundlagen der Arithmetik. Eine logisch mathematische Untersuchung über den Begriff der Zahl*. Breslau: Wilhelm Koebner Verlag.

Hale, Bob 1979: "Strawson, Geach and Dummett on Singular Terms". *Synthese* 42, 275–95.

— 1987: *Abstract Objects*. Oxford: Basil Blackwell.

— 1994: "Dummett's Critique of Wright's Attempt to Resusciate Frege." *Philosophia Mathematica* 3, 122–47. Reprinted in: Hale & Wright, 2001.

— 1995: "Singular Terms (2)". In: Brian McGuiness & Gianluigi Olivieri (eds), *The Philosophy of Michael Dummett*. Dordrecht: Kluwer, 17–44. Reprinted in: Hale and Wright, 2001.

— 1996: "Singular Terms (1)". In: Matthias Schirn (ed.), *Frege: Importance and Legacy*. Berlin, New York: Walter de Gruyter, 438–57. Reprinted in: Hale & Wright, 2001.

— 2000: "Reals by Abstraction". *Philosophia Mathematica* 8, 100–123.

Hale, Bob & Wright, Crispin 2000: "Implicit Definition and the a priori". In: Paul Boghossian & Christopher Peacocke (eds), *New Essays on the A Priori*. Oxford: Oxford University Press, 286–319. Reprinted in: Hale & Wright, 2001.

— 2001: *The Reason's Proper Study: Essays towards a Neo-Fregean Philosophy of Mathematics*. Oxford: Oxford University Press.

— 2002: "Benacerraf's Dilemma Revisited". *European Journal of Philosophy* 10(1), 101–129.

Keefe, Rosanna & Smith, Peter 1997: *Vagueness: A Reader*. Cambridge, Mass: MIT Press.

Linnebo, Øystein, "Platonism in the Philosophy of Mathematics." In: Edward N. Zalta (ed.), *The Stanford Encyclopedia of Philosophy* (Winter 2013 Edition). URL = <http://plato.stanford.edu/archives/win2013/entries/platonism-mathematics/>.

MacBride, Fraser 2003: "Speaking with Shadows: A Study of Neo-Fregeanism". *British Journal for the Philosophy of Science* 54, 103–63.

Quine, Willard Van Orman 1935: "Truth by Convention". In: Filmer Northrop & Mason Gross (eds), *Philosophical Essays for Alfred North Whitehead*. New York: Longmans. Reprinted in: Quine, 1966.

— 1960: "Carnap on Logical Truth". *Synthese* 12(4), 350–74. Reprinted in: Quine, 1966.

Quine, Willard Van Orman 1966: *The Ways of Paradox*. New York: Random House.
Rosen, Gideon 1993: "The Refutation of Nominalism". *Philosophical Topics* 21, 149–86.
Shapiro, Shapiro 1998: "Logical Consequence: Models and Modality". In: Matthias Schirn(ed), *Philosophy of Mathematics Today*. Oxford: Oxford University Press, 131–156.
Wetzel, Lisa 1990: "Dummett's Criteria for Singular Terms". *Mind* 99, 239–64.
Williamson, Timothy 1988: "Review of B. Hale, 1987, Abstract Objects". *Mind* 98, 487–90.
Wright, Crispin 1983: *Frege's Conception of Numbers as Objects*. Aberdeen: Aberdeen University Press.
— 1995: "Critical Notice of Michael Dummett's Frege: Philosophy ofMathematics". *Philosophical Books*. Reprinted in: Schirn, 1998 and in: Hale & Wright, 2001.
— 1998a: "On the (Harmless) Impredicativity of Hume's Principle". In:Matthias Schirn (ed), *Philosophy of Mathematics Today*. Oxford: Oxford University Press, 339–368. Reprinted in: Hale & Wright, 2001.
— 1998b: "Why Frege Did Not Deserve his Granum Salis: a Note on theParadox of the 'Concept Horse'". *Grazer Philosophische Studien* 55, 239–63. Reprinted in: Hale and Wright, 2001.
— 2016: "Abstraction and Epistemic Entitlement: On the EpistemologicalStatus of Hume's Principle". In Philip A. Ebert & Marcus Rossberg (eds), *Abstractionism*. Oxford: Oxford University Press.

WHAT IS WRONG WITH CLASSICAL NEGATION?

Nils KÜRBIS
Birkbeck, University of London

> Für die Negation liegen die
> Verhältnisse nicht so einfach.[1]
> *Gentzen*

Abstract

The focus of this paper are Dummett's meaning-theoretical arguments against classical logic based on considerations about the meaning of negation. Using Dummettian principles, I shall outline three such arguments, of increasing strength, and show that they are unsuccessful by giving responses to each argument on behalf of the classical logician. What is crucial is that in responding to these arguments a classicist need not challenge any of the basic assumptions of Dummett's outlook on the theory of meaning. In particular, I shall grant Dummett his general bias towards verificationism, encapsulated in the slogan 'meaning is use'. The second general assumption I see no need to question is Dummett's particular breed of molecularism. *Some* of Dummett's assumptions will have to be given up, if classical logic is to be vindicated in his meaning-theoretical framework. A major result of this paper will be that *the meaning of negation cannot be defined by rules of inference in the Dummettian framework.*[2]

Keywords: Proof-theoretic semantics, harmony, negation, ex falso quodlibet, compositionality, molecular theories of meaning

---

1. 'The situation is not so easy for negation.' (Gentzen 1936, 511)
2. This paper has been with me for a while. Many people have read or heard versions of it and contributed with their comments. Instead of trying to list them all, which would undoubtedly lead to unintended omissions, I'd like to single out two philosophers to whom I am particularly indebted. Bernhard Weiss, to whom everything I know about Dummett can be traced, and Keith Hossack, my *Doktorvater*, for his robust philosophical challenges. This paper would not have been written without their advice and encouragement. I would also like to thank the referees for *Grazer Philosophische Studien*, whose constructive criticism resulted in a substantial improvement of this paper.

1. Introduction

Dummett's meaning-theoretical arguments against classical logic are divided into two kinds. One kind comprises arguments based on the nature of knowing and understanding a language: here belong the manifestability and the acquisition arguments. These arguments aim to establish that the nature of speakers' understanding of a language does not warrant the assumption that every sentence is determinately either true or false. It is widely agreed that they are either unsuccessful[3] or too underdeveloped to carry the force they are intended to carry—the latter point being attested to by Dummett himself, who admits that it is far from a settled issue what full manifestability amounts to.[4]

The other kind comprises arguments based on how the meanings of the logical constants are to be determined in the theory of meaning. They are the focus of the present paper. Using Dummettian principles, I shall outline three such arguments, of increasing strength, and show that they are unsuccessful by giving responses to each argument on behalf of the classicist[5].

It is crucial that in responding to these arguments a classicist need not challenge any of the basic assumptions of Dummett's outlook on the theory of meaning. In particular, I shall grant Dummett his general bias towards verificationism, encapsulated in the slogan 'meaning is use'. The second general assumption I see no need to question is Dummett's particular breed of molecularism. The point of the present paper is to investigate how, accepting these Dummettian assumptions, the classicist can counter Dummett's arguments.

Some of Dummett's assumptions will have to be given up, if classical logic is to be vindicated in his meaning-theoretical framework. I will argue that *the meaning of negation cannot be defined by rules of inference in the Dummettian framework*.

As Dummett's project is well known, the discussion of his views on the theory of meaning remains deliberately concise.

---

3. Transposing Alexander Miller's arguments from the semantic realist to the adherent of classical logic (Miller 2002, 2003).
4. Cf. the 'Preface' to (Dummett 1991).
5. In defiance of the OED, where 'classicist' is reserved for persons who study Classics or followers of Classicism, I shall use this term to refer to adherents of classical logic.

2. *tertium non datur*

2.1 *Against tertium non datur*

Dummett rejects holism, the view that the meaning of a word is determined by the whole language in which it occurs, as well as atomism, the view that the meaning of a word can be determined individually. In received terminology, the principle of compositionality states that the meaning of a syntactically complex expression depends on the meanings of its constituent expressions and the way they are assembled. Dummett argues for a more substantial principle, which he calls by the same name. 'The principle of compositionality is not the mere truism, which even a holist must acknowledge, that the meaning of a sentence is determined by its composition. Its bite comes from the thesis that the understanding of a word consists in the ability to understand characteristic members of a particular range of sentences containing that word.' (Dummett 1993, 225) The notion of complexity on which a molecular theory of meaning is built cannot be equated with syntactic complexity, but characterises semantic features of expressions. There are expressions an understanding of which requires an understanding of others first. For instance, whereas understanding the terminology of the theory of the colour sphere presupposes an understanding of colour words, the converse is not true: a speaker may be proficient in using colour words like 'red', 'green', 'yellow' and 'blue' without understanding the terms 'pure', 'mixed' and 'complementary colour' or what is meant by 'saturation', 'hue' and 'brightness'. The latter expressions are semantically more complex than the former. As Dummett puts it, a relation of dependence of meaning holds between them. 'What the principle of compositionality essentially requires is that the relation of dependence between [sets of] expressions and [sets of] sentence-forms be asymmetric.' (Dummett 1993, 223) The qualification 'sets of' is needed because there may be collections of expressions that, although they must form surveyable sets, can only be learned simultaneously; according to Dummett, this is true for simple colour words (*ibid.*). A theory of meaning employs the relation of dependence to impose on the expressions of the language 'a hierarchical structure deviating only slightly from being a partial ordering' (*ibid.*). It thereby exhibits how the language is learnable step by step. In learning a language, a speaker works his way up the hierarchy from semantically less complex to semantically more complex expressions. Mastering a stage in this process is to master everything a speaker needs to know about the meanings of the expressions constituting that stage, and it does not alter the speaker's understanding of the meanings of expressions constituting stages lower in the hierarchy. This is Dummett's molecularism in the theory of meaning. To avoid confusion with received terminology, I shall avoid using 'compositionality' where the semantic notion of complexity is concerned and instead use 'molecularity'.

Applying molecularity to proof-theory and combining it with the verificationism derived from the principle that meaning is use, according to Dummett a proof should never need to appeal to sentences more complex than that which is proved. It should be possible to transform any proof into one which satises this requirement. A speaker following a proof should always be able to work his way up from *less* complex assumptions to a *more* complex conclusion, where of course intermediate steps down through less complex sentences are allowed on the way up. Dummett puts forward the fundamental assumption of the proof-theoretic justification of deduction: 'if we have a valid argument for a complex statement, we can construct a valid argument for it which finishes with an application of one of the introduction rules governing its principal operator.' (Dummett 1993, 254) Leaving out the technical details, the fundamental assumption ensures that we can always construct proofs in such a way that the sentences occurring in the proof can be ordered by the relation of dependence of meaning, as required by molecularity, in such a way that the conclusion occupies the highest point in the hierarchy.[6]

With this material, Dummett can give a compelling argument against classical logic on meaning-theoretical grounds. I shall follow traditional terminology and call $A \vee \neg A$ *tertium non datur*, which deviates from

---

6. According to Dummett, the fundamental assumption applies not only to arguments which are proofs, but also to the more general case of deductions with undischarged premises, which, as Dummett acknowledges, meets some formidable difficulties (Dummett 1993, Chapter 12). These difficulties are irrelevant to the arguments to be given here, as they only require that the fundamental assumption applies to theorems, in which case it is provable for intuitionist logic and some formulations of classical logic. In another paper I argue that, quite independently of the present considerations, it is best to restrict the fundamental assumption in this way (Kürbis 2012). Strictly speaking, we should also make a distinction between 'argument', 'canonical proof' and 'demonstration', but this introduces a complexity unnecessary in the present context. Arguments may contain 'boundary rules', which are rules allowing the deduction of atomic sentences from other atomic sentences, as well as arbitrary inferences (Dummett 1993, 254). Canonical proofs and demonstrations are essentially special cases thereof, formalised in a system of natural deduction satisfying Dummettian criteria.

Dummett's terminology. A proof of *tertium non datur* in the system of classical logic formalised in (Prawitz 1965) proceeds as follows:[7]

$$\cfrac{\cfrac{\neg(A \vee \neg A)\quad \cfrac{\cfrac{\overline{\neg(A \vee \neg A)}^{\,2}\quad \cfrac{\overline{\neg A}^{\,1}}{A \vee \neg A}}{\bot}}{A \vee \neg A}^{\,1}}{\bot}}{A \vee \neg A}^{\,2}$$

The proof violates molecularity: the less complex $A \vee \neg A$ is deduced from the more complex discharged assumption $\neg(A \vee \neg A)$. No proof of $A \vee \neg A$ which would satisfy Dummett's criteria can be given. For how should such a proof of $A \vee \neg A$ proceed? By molecularity and the fundamental assumption, $A \vee \neg A$ would have to be derived from A or from $\neg A$. Whichever it is, it must come from assumptions that are discharged in the process of the argument. It cannot be A, for this may be an atomic sentence and no atomic sentence follows from no premises at all.[8] It cannot be $\neg A$ either, for, if A is atomic, neither does $\neg A$ follow from no premises at all.[9] Hence it is not possible to meet Dummett's criteria on molecular theories of meaning *and* accept $A \vee \neg A$ as a theorem.[10]

This argument against classical negation is remarkable. The main assumption it is based on is that a theory of meaning should be molecular, which is a very plausible assumption. It is not an argument that Dummett gives himself, but, being based purely upon Dummettian considerations, it is one that he could give, in particular as he thinks that double negation elimination or an equivalent classical negation rule like *consequentia mira-*

---

7. I'll discuss various ways of formalising classical logic in Prawitz' system in due course and show what is wrong with them on the Dummettian plan. We can exclude ways of formalising logics that Dummett excludes, such as multiple conclusion logics.
8. If A is not something like *verum*, but it is clear enough how the point is to be taken.
9. If A is not something like *falsum*, *cf.* the previous footnote.
10. For special areas of enquiry one may be able to show that either A or $\neg A$, as is the case in intuitionist arithmetic for atomic A. However, this is not a question of *logic*: it makes assumptions concerning the subject matter of the atomic sentences, and logic makes no such assumptions.

bilis, from $\Gamma, \neg A \vdash \bot$ to infer $\Gamma \vdash A$, violate constraints on molecularity. It is an argument that is very strong indeed.[11]

2.2 *A classicist response*

The appeal to molecularity in the argument against *tertium non datur* assumes that $A \vee \neg A$ and $\neg(A \vee \neg A)$ are of different semantic complexity. It is a fair question to ask—whether one is a classicist or not—what it is that a speaker needs to understand in order to understand $\neg(A \vee \neg A)$ that she does not need to understand in order to understand $A \vee \neg A$. On the face of it, there is nothing in one that is not in the other. To understand $A \vee \neg A$ and $\neg(A \vee \neg A)$, one needs to understand $\neg, \vee$ and that A stands for a sentence. Dummett introduces two notions of complexity: syntactic complexity, related to what is normally called the principle of compositionality, and semantic complexity, his notion of molecularity. The two notions do not coincide. For the argument against *tertium non datur* to go through, it has to be assumed that the fact that $\neg(A \vee \neg A)$ contains $A \vee \neg A$ as a proper subformula, and is therefore syntactically more complex, carries over to their respective semantic complexities. I shall argue that this assumption is unmotivated.

Consider what Dummett says is involved in understanding 'or'. 'On a compositional [i.e. molecular] meaning-theory, to know the meaning of 'or', for example, is to be able to derive, from the meanings of any sentences A and B, the meaning of ⌜A or B⌝ […] To understand ⌜A or B⌝, therefore, you must (i) observe the composition of the sentence, (ii) know what 'or' means, (iii) know what A and B mean.' (Dummett 1993, 222) Decomposing clauses (ii) and (iii) in the cases of $A \vee \neg A$ and $\neg(A \vee \neg A)$ end in the same final components: in each case you need to know what $\vee, \neg$ and A mean.

Arguably, clause (i) does not impart semantic complexity either. I cannot just observe the composition of a sentence in the abstract, as it were:

---

11. It rules out even logics in which negation is conservative over the positive fragment, such as the relevant logic **R**. According to Belnap, responding to (Prior 1961), conservativeness is a requirement for the *existence* of a constant (Belnap 1962, 133f.). This is not sufficient to ensure that the constant is a respectable one on Dummett's account, as other meaning-theoretical constraints have to be satised, too. Hence someone following Peter Milne's suggestion of viewing *consequentia mirabilis* as an introduction rule for A still needs to answer Dummett's molecularity constraint, as Milne himself notes (Milne 1994, 58f.). The present paper can be seen as providing Milne with a solution to this problem.

understanding the composition is essentially tied to an understanding of the parts and how they are pieced together. To understand ∨, I need to understand that it takes two sentences and forms a sentence out of them. I also need to understand the principles of inference governing it. As there are two introduction rules for ∨, my understanding guarantees that I understand that the order of the sub-sentences plays a role in the composition, even though the two options are logically equivalent. As another example, take ⊃: understanding this connective involves understanding that it forms a sentence out of two sentences and the rules of inference governing it. The latter guarantee that my understanding also involves an understanding that the meaning of the resulting sentence is different depending on which sentence I put to the left and which one to the right of ⊃. How to compose sentences with these constants is an essential part of understanding them. It comes together with an understanding of what ∨ or ⊃ mean that they put together sentences in a certain way, which results in the sentences having a certain composition.

In addition, the meanings of the logical constants are given in a completely general way. Concerning the understanding of logical constants, Dummett writes that 'the understanding of a logical constant *consists* in the ability to understand any sentence of which it is the principal operator: the understanding of a sentence in which it occurs otherwise than as the principal operator *depends on*, but does not go to constitute, an understanding of the constant.' (Dummett 1993, 224) The rules governing it tell us how to proceed when the constant applies to any sentences whatsoever. If I understand an operator and can apply it in one case (e.g. ¬A), I can also be expected to be able to apply it in any other case (e.g. ¬(A ∨ ¬A)), given I understand the rest of the context, which *ex hypothesi* is so in the case of *tertium non datur*, as ∨ is understood. Of course we need to observe how the components are pieced together. But in piecing them together in one way or other, no new conceptual resources are required.

Following this line of reasoning, the classicist can point out that in fact the proof of *tertium non datur* does not violate molecularity. The difference in the syntactic complexity between A ∨ ¬A and ¬(A ∨ ¬A) does not carry over to the semantic level. Exactly the same conceptual resources are needed to understand either of them.

Thus the classicist has a straightforward response to the Dummettian argument against *tertium non datur*. It proceeds entirely on Dummettian grounds, appealing only to principles that Dummett himself puts forward. It has the further implication of revealing the fundamental assumption to be an excessive requirement, if, as Dummett demands, it is applied strictly to the main operator of a theorem.

The phenomenon that syntactic complexity doesn't carry over to semantic complexity is more widespread than just the logical constants. Consider 'Fred paints the wall in complementary colours'. This is syntactically less complex than 'Fred paints the wall in red and green, or blue and orange, or purple and yellow'. However, it is semantically more complex, as I cannot understand the concept 'complementary colour' without understanding simple colour words. Similarly, Dummett suggests that 'child', 'boy' and 'girl' are expressions that occupy the same point in the partial ordering that dependence of meaning imposes on the expressions of the language. They can only be learnt together, where some logical relations between them need to be recognised as well (Dummett 1993, 267). If this is so, then, even though it is syntactically more complex, 'Hilary is a boy or a girl' is semantically as complex as 'Hilary is a child'.

2.3 Conclusion

Although unsuccessful, the Dummettian argument against *tertium non datur* is significant as it is an attempt to formulate an argument against classical logic purely on the basis of very general considerations about the form a theory of meaning has to take. It relies on the assumption that the difference in the syntactic complexity between $A \vee \neg A$ and $\neg(A \vee \neg A)$ carries over to the semantic level. The classicist can respond by denying that this is so.

The classicist response is not based on any specifically classical principles. In particular, it makes no reference to the fact that classical logic does not need $\vee$ as a primitive, which the Dummettian can counter by arguing that as ordinary language has an undefined 'or', logic should have $\vee$ undefined, too. The core and motivation of the classicist response can be accepted by philosophers of any logical bias. The argument against *tertium non datur* aims to establish that something is wrong with classical logic, if the framework of a Dummettian theory of meaning is assumed. The classicist response does not proceed by establishing that something is wrong with Dummett's favourite, intuitionist logic, but only that the argument fails to show that something is wrong with classical logic: we have not been given good reasons to believe that classical logic does not fit into the Dummettian framework.

Philosophy being what it is, straightforward arguments and simple responses won't settle the issue. In the next section, I shall give a second

Dummettian argument against classical negation that aims to establish that negation in general does add to the semantic complexity of sentences, and I shall provide a corresponding classicist response.

3. *Classical negation rules*

3.1 *Against rules yielding classical negation*

The Dummettian argument against *tertium non datur* focussed on a specific application of classical negation rules. The classicist response counters that this application cannot be objectionable on Dummettian grounds. The Dummettian should now focus more generally on the effect of rules that, when added to intuitionist logic, yield classical logic.

To illustrate the line of argument, assume classical logic is formalised by adding double negation elimination to intuitionist logic with the following rules for negation introduction and elimination and *ex falso quodlibet*:

$$\dfrac{\overline{A}^{\,i}\;\;\;\Xi\;\;\;\bot}{\neg A}^{\,i} \qquad \dfrac{A\quad \neg A}{\bot} \qquad \dfrac{\bot}{B}$$

I'll discuss other ways of extending intuitionist to classical logic in due course.

To establish that these rules violate general constraints imposed on the theory of meaning, the Dummettian needs to point out that there are sentences B not containing negation which can be established as true *only* by using double negation elimination, such as Pierce's Law $((A \supset B) \supset A) \supset A$. Then the inference of B from $\neg\neg B$ would, on Dummettian principles, be constitutive of the meaning of B, because it licenses uses of B that are not possible independently of this move. Hence the meaning of B would depend on the meaning of $\neg\neg B$. But there is a component in $\neg\neg B$ the meaning of which has to be acquired independently of B, i.e. negation. To acquire an understanding of the meaning of negation, a speaker needs to acquire an understanding of the rules of inference for negation, which he doesn't have to know in order to know B. This is a case where syntactic and semantic complexity go hand in hand. For the Dummettian, $\neg\neg B$ counts not only as syntactically more complex than

B, but also as more complex in the semantic sense. Thus by molecularity, the meaning of $\neg\neg B$ is dependent on the meaning of B and negation. This is a circular dependence of meaning: a speaker who wishes to command an understanding of B would first have to command an understanding of $\neg\neg B$, which, however, cannot be achieved independently of mastery of the meaning of B. A speaker could not break into the circle and learn the meaning of B. B could have no place in the partial ordering that the relation of dependence of meaning imposes on the language. Hence B cannot have a stable meaning at all. It follows that double negation elimination should be rejected, as it is incompatible with Dummett's molecularism and his interpretation of the principle that meaning is use.[12]

In deriving a problematic sentence A of the kind we are interested in, double negation elimination need not be applied in the final step, so that the whole sentence to be derived is its conclusion. It may instead be applied to deduce a proper subsentence B of A. There will then still be a sentence that, in the process of the deduction, can only be derived by deriving its double negation first. What affects the part affects the whole: A cannot have a stable meaning if its subsentence B does not have one. Moreover, such a proof of A can always be transformed into one in which double negation elimination is the final step, and, for reasons to be explained later in this section, they both have to count equally as canonical verifications, and the problem that affects the one affects the other.

It is clear that what applies to double negation elimination equally applies to other rules for classical negation. The observation at the basis of the argument against double negation elimination—that there are sentences B not containing negation that can only be verified by apply-

---

12. It is worth reflecting whether there are examples of non-logical sentences not containing negation that can only be verified by double negation elimination, if classical logic is used, i.e. whether the non-conservativeness of classical negation over the positive fragment of intuitionist logic applies also to non-logical sentences. Maybe the following is an example. Consider an embryo. Let's call it Hilary. An intuitionist would resist the temptation of asserting that Hilary is either a boy or a girl, as neither disjunct can yet be verified. But consider 'Hilary is neither a boy nor a girl'. Intuitionistically, this is equivalent to 'Hilary is not a boy and not a girl'. But an intuitionist might accept that if a child is not a boy, then it is a girl: arguably, verifying that a child is not a boy just is or must proceed via verifying that it is a girl. Hence if Hilary is neither a boy nor a girl, Hilary is a girl and not a girl, which is impossible. Hence, the intuitionist can conclude that it is not the case that Hilary is neither a boy or a girl. The classicist would proceed to apply double negation elimination to conclude that Hilary is either a boy or a girl, even though there is no direct verification of the sentence. If this is plausible, then 'Hilary is either a boy or a girl' is an example of a sentence which, if classical logic is used, can only be verified by verifying its double negation first.

ing double negation elimination—generalises. As classical negation is not conservative over the positive fragment of intuitionist logic, any rules for classical negation will enable us to derive sentences not containing negation using sentences containing negation. The Dummettian observes that, if classical negation rules are employed, there are sentences A not containing negation that can only be verified by a process that at some point appeals to the negation $\neg B$ of a subsentence B of A (not necessarily a proper subsentence). To understand $\neg B$ a speaker needs to understand something he does not need to understand in order to understand B: negation. Classical negation rules affect the use of B, as they affect the conditions under which it is assertible, and thus its meaning. This, once more, produces a circular dependence of meaning, just as in the case of double negation elimination.

There are other ways of extending intuitionist logic to classical logic than adding double negation elimination. We could add rules for implication, such as Pierce's Rule:

$$\dfrac{\overline{A \supset B}^{\,i}}{\begin{array}{c}\Pi\\ A\end{array}}\,i$$

This rule violates molecularity. If A can only be verified by appeal to this rule, then the application of the rule would be constitutive of its meaning. But $A \supset B$ occurs in an undischarged assumption, so a speaker applying the rule needs to understand that sentence in order to be able to do so. However, the meaning of $A \supset B$ depends on the meaning of A. Again, there is a circular dependence of meaning between A and $A \supset B$.

If negation is defined in terms of $\bot$ and $\supset$, Peirce's Rule generalises a classical negation rule:

$$\dfrac{\overline{\neg A}^{\,i}}{\begin{array}{c}\Pi\\ A\end{array}}\,i$$

Even keeping $\neg$ primitive, the special case is no improvement on the general case: if A can only be verified by appeal to that rule, then the meaning of A is dependent on the meaning of $\neg A$, which appears in an undischarged premise, and conversely, $\neg A$ is dependent on the meaning of A. Again there is a circular dependence of meaning. The same counts for *consequentia mirabilis*:

$$\frac{\overline{\neg A}^{\,i}}{\begin{array}{c}\Pi\\ \bot\\ \hline A\end{array}}i$$

Another strategy is to add dilemma:

$$\frac{\overline{A}\quad \overline{\neg A}^{\,i}}{\begin{array}{cc}\Pi & \Sigma\\ B & B\end{array}}\;i\atop B$$

Here the situation is slightly more complicated, but essentially the same. Any deduction that ends with an application of dilemma can be transformed into one that appeals to $\neg B$:

$$\frac{\overline{A}^{\,1}}{\begin{array}{c}\Pi\\ \overline{\neg B}^{\,2}\quad B\\ \hline \bot\\ \hline \neg A\end{array}}1\atop \begin{array}{c}\Sigma\\ \overline{B}^{\,2}\quad B\\ \hline B\end{array}2$$

The case we are interested in is where the final application of dilemma was part of a canonical verification of B. The transformed deduction contains a formula, $\neg B$, that the original one did not contain, and it contains additional applications of negation introduction and elimination. However, both deductions employ exactly the same conceptual resources. To follow the original proof, the speaker needs to understand negation.

So he understands $\neg B$, as the understanding of negation, being a logical constant, is general. For the same reason, the additional applications of rules for negation only draw on resources the speaker who can follow the original deduction already needs to command. The transformed deduction may contain a maximal formula, if $\neg A$ is the major premise of negation elimination in Σ. It can be removed: the conclusion of the rule will be $\bot$, and we can move the deduction leading to the minor premise on top of A in Π. If there is no such deduction, the case is trivial. The resulting deduction is still a deduction of B via $\neg B$. Thus there is no reason not to count the transformed deduction also as a canonical verification of B. Dummett does not require that every sentence has at most one canonical verification. Quite to the contrary. Understanding a sentence involves a grasp of the wealth of conditions under which it counts as conclusively verified. Each derivation must count as equally constitutive of the meaning of B, and once more we have a circular dependence of meaning, where B depends on $\neg B$, but $\neg B$ depends on B.

We can generalise dilemma with the following rule:[13]

$$\cfrac{\cfrac{\overline{A \supset B}^{\,i} \quad \overline{B \supset C}^{\,i}}{\begin{array}{cc} \Pi & \Sigma \\ D & D \end{array}}}{D}\,i$$

A deduction that ends in an application of this rule can be transformed into one in which D is a subformula of a discharged assumption:

---

13. We get dilemma by replacing A with $\top$ and C with $\bot$. Deleting $A \supset$ gives yet another rule that yields classical negation. It is unacceptable to the Dummettian for similar reasons as the general version.

$$\cfrac{\cfrac{\overline{\top \supset D}^{\,2} \quad \overline{\top}}{D} \quad \cfrac{\cfrac{\overline{D \supset C}^{\,2} \quad \cfrac{\cfrac{\overline{B}^{\,1}}{A \supset B}}{\Pi}}{\cfrac{C}{B \supset C}^{\,1}}}{\Sigma}}{D}_{\,2}$$

Instead of $\top$, we could use an arbitrary, but suitably chosen tautology, say $D \supset D$. We could, indeed, also replace $\top$ with other suitably chosen sentences, in particular sentences E such that the meanings of sentences occurring in the original deduction depend on the meaning of E in the partial ordering that dependence of meaning imposes on the sentences of a language in a molecular theory of meaning. As in the case of dilemma, the transformed deduction uses exactly the same conceptual resources as the original deduction. Maximal formulas arising from the transformation can be removed. If the former was a canonical deduction of D, so is the latter. We get a circular dependence of meaning: D depends on $C \supset D$, which in turn depends on D, violating molecularity.

Adding corresponding axioms instead of rules cannot make a difference to the situation, as they are equivalent. Besides, axioms, according to Dummett, count as introduction rules. They introduce grounds for asserting sentences that are not matched by the consequences of asserting them, as laid down by the elimination rules for the main connective of the axiom. Axioms, then, immediately violate Dummett's verificationism.

In this section, I have only discussed specific cases of rules. It would be desirable to establish a general result to the effect that any rules that yield classical logic, when added to intuitionist logic, violate molecularity. The cases discussed are, however, the most prominent ones and are sufficiently varied to shift the burden of proof. Once more, we can describe Dummett as formulating a challenge: find rules that yield classical negation that won't violate general constraints on the theory of meaning. For the present purposes, we can leave matters here. I shall go on to discuss a classicist response to the concerns of the present section that will exonerate the classicist from answering this renewed challenge.

To finish, here is a conjecture for a formal result that I leave for another occasion: A deduction Π ending with an application of a rule that yields classical logic can be transformed into a deduction Π' of the same conclusion with the following properties: a) Π' finishes with an application of the same rule as Π; b) the conclusion of Π' occurs as a proper subformula of a discharged premise; c) only rules applied in Π are applied in Π'; d) formulas in Π' not occurring in Π are composed of subformulas of formulas occuring in Π. The idea is the following. For introduction and elimination rules to be in harmony, they need to full certain constraints. The resulting logic is intuitionist. To extend it to classical logic, rules need to be added that discharge assumptions containing logical constants, an option Dummett excludes (Dummett 1993, 297). Given further constraints on such rules, a general procedure can be specied that transforms deductions in the desired way. Thus any such rule violates molecularity.

3.2 *Another classicist response*

To counter the argument against rules yielding classical logic, it suffices to argue that classical negation rules do not, in fact, violate molecularity. What is needed is a further assumption, one that is very plausible from the classical perspective, but not inherently classicist: although $\neg A$ is *syntactically* more complex than A, this does not carry over to the crucial *semantic* notion of complexity at the foundation of Dummett's molecularism.

Peter Geach has proposed a view on negation which has the desired consequences. Geach holds that an understanding of negation and an understanding of affirmation[14] cannot be separated from each other. A speaker cannot understand Fa without understanding $\neg Fa$ and conversely: 'they go inseparately together—*eadem est scientia oppositorum*.' (Geach 1972, 79) Following Geach, I shall use 'predicate' to mean not a predicate letter, but a meaningful expression of a language, or alternatively 'concept'. Someone understanding a predicate needs to be able to distinguish between things to which it applies and things to which it does not apply. Understanding a predicate enables a speaker to draw this distinction. Thus understanding a predicate endows a speaker with a grasp of affirma-

---

14. Affirmation is not to be confused with assertion, which is a speech act. Historically, 'position' has also been used to denote the opposite of negation.

tion as well as negation. Consequently, 'the understanding of "not male" is no more complex than that of "male".' (*ibid.*) To grasp a concept is inseparable from grasping its negation, as 'knowing what is red and what is not are inseparable.' (Geach 1971, 25) A speaker cannot acquire a grasp of one without acquiring a grasp of the other: they are learnt together. Hence, according to Geach, a sentence and its negation are of the same semantic complexity.[15]

If the classicist adopts Geach's account of negation, there is an answer to the molecularity challenge posed by the argument against rules yielding classical negation. If negation and affirmation go inseparably together, then diagnosing a difference in the complexities of A and $\neg A$ relies on a misconception: it is wrong to measure their semantic complexity by observing that one contains a sentential operator in principal position that the other lacks. As a speaker acquires an understanding of both simultaneously, the same conceptual resources are required in understanding A and understanding $\neg A$. Transposing Geach's ideas to the Dummettian molecular theory of meaning, A and $\neg A$ occupy the same position in the partial ordering that dependence of meaning imposes on a language. Thus they have the same semantic complexity. If the sense of an expression is something a speaker has to know about the expression in order to be able to use it, then a theory of meaning along Geach's lines would specify simultaneously the senses of A and its negation $\neg A$. Correspondingly, establishing $\neg A$ as true is an operation of the same complexity as establishing A as true. Consequently, the argument against classical negation rules loses its force: a verification of B that proceeds via $\neg B$ does not result in a circular dependence of meaning, and hence unintelligibility, even if B does not contain negation and cannot be verified otherwise.

This completes the classicist response to the Dummettian argument against rules yielding classical negation. There are, however, no obvious reasons why Geach's view on negation should be restricted to the clas-

---

15. Although Geach puts his point in terms of predicate negation, it carries over to sentential negation and was certainly intended to do so. This is particularly clear in the present context, as Dummett and, according to his interpretation, Frege would call $\neg F\xi$ the negation of the predicate $F\xi$ only in a derivative way. Strictly speaking, there is no predicate negation, according to Frege/Dummett. Negation is a function, and functions always have objects as values, whereas predicate negation would take functions as values (Dummett 1981, 40ff.). $\neg F\xi$ is not constructed from $F\xi$ by applying negation, but in the same way as every predicate: from a sentence by omitting some occurrences of a name: from the sentence Fa we omit the name a to get the predicate $F\xi$, we apply negation to the sentence Fa to get $\neg Fa$ and drop a from it to get the predicate $\neg F\xi$. In the final analysis, any talk of predicate negation is explicable in terms of sentential negation.

sicist. It is quite neutral. An intuitionist might accept it, too. The point that a sentence and its negation are of equal semantic complexity can be motivated independently of which rules negation is subject to. Initially at least, Geach makes no reference to classical logic.[16]

3.3 Conclusion

The argument against classical negation rested on the observation that, if classical logic is used, there are sentences not containing negation that can be verified only by a process that appeals to rules yielding classical negation, and that this leads to a violation of molecularity, due to the nature of those rules. The classicist response rested on the assumption that a sentence and its negation are of equal semantic complexity. This may be controversial. But as with the classicist response to the argument against *tertium non datur*, although this assumption is particularly attractive for classicists like Geach, it is not one that actually depends on any specically classicist assumptions. An intuitionist could adopt it, too.

The next Dummettian argument I shall consider aims at establishing that the negation of a sentence must be semantically more complex than the sentence itself. It differs from the argument against *tertium non datur* and rules yielding classical negation in that it not only attempts to show that something is wrong with classical logic, but also that intuitionist logic is the right logic.

4. *ex falso quodlibet*

4.1 *Negation according to Dummett and Prawitz*

The two Dummettian arguments against classical logic given so far fail to establish the desired conclusion that something is wrong with classical

---

16. This is not affected by Geach's illustration of his view, an obvious reference to Frege's metaphor of concepts with sharp boundaries (Frege 1998, Vol. II: §56): 'A predicate may be represented by a closed line on a surface, and predicating it of an object be represented by placing the point representing the object on one or other side of this line. A predicate and its negation will then clearly be represented by one and the same line; and there can be no question of logical priority as between the inside and the outside of the line, which inseparately coexist.' (Geach 1972, 79) According to this picture, $\neg\neg A$ has the same content as A. This view is not needed to counter the molecularity challenge. Geach notices that the picture is problematic for vague predicates. It is only an illustration and not essential to Geach's philosophical point.

logic. Dummett needs a more forceful argument using more resources than just general constraints on the theory of meaning. The argument I shall turn to now is based on a very substantial additional theory, the *proof-theoretic justification of deduction*. Its core tenet is that the meanings of the logical constants, and thus negation, are to be defined by rules of inference governing them. It is an argument which not only is intended to point towards a deficiency in classical logic but also aims to establish that intuitionist logic is the correct logic.

Dummett argues that the meanings of logical constants should be given by self-justifying rules of inference governing them. To exclude connectives like Prior's *tonk*, these rules are required to be in harmony. For the present purposes, I do not need to go into the details of Dummett's account and can remain fairly informal about this notion.[17] Dummett demands that there be harmony between the canonical grounds of an assertion of a sentence with a main connective $*$ and the consequences of accepting it as true. Molecularity plays a role in motivating harmony: learning the meaning of logical connectives does not affect the meanings of expressions you have already learnt (nor, indeed, does what you have already learnt affect their meanings). Dummett claims that if the procedure of the proof-theoretic justification of deduction is followed, the meanings of the logical constants are given independently of a notion of truth that prejudges issues between classicists and intuitionists. The logic which turns out to be the justified one is the correct logic.[18]

Dummett argues that the negation operator should be defined in terms of implication and *falsum*, $\neg A =_{def.} A \supset \bot$, as considerations of rules for an undefined negation operator show. There are two common options for the introduction rule. The first option is that $\neg A$ follows if A entails a contradiction:

$$\cfrac{\cfrac{\overline{A}^{\,i} \quad \overline{A}^{\,i}}{\begin{array}{cc} \Pi & \Xi \\ B & \neg B \end{array}}}{\neg A}\,i$$

---

17. I give formally precise definitions of harmony and stability in (Kürbis 2013), which work by specifying how to read off introduction from elimination rules and conversely.
18. For details, *cf.* (Dummett 1993, chapters 11–13).

It can hardly be claimed that the meaning of negation is defined by this rule: negation is already used in the premises.[19] Dummett himself employs a rule which suffers from the same inadequacy (Dummett 1993, 291):

$$\frac{\overline{A}^{\,i}}{}$$
$$\Xi$$
$$\frac{\neg A}{\neg A}\,i$$

A more promising option is to employ the introduction rule that $\neg A$ may be derived if A entails *falsum*:

$$\overline{A}^{\,i}$$
$$\Xi$$
$$\frac{\bot}{\neg A}\,i$$

$\bot$ is governed by *ex falso quodlibet*, where B may be restricted to atomic formulas:

$$\frac{\bot}{B}$$

Negation introduction is harmonious with the rule *ex contradictione falsum*, needed for a complete account of negation:

$$\frac{A \qquad \neg A}{\bot}$$

An attempt at defining the meaning of negation in terms of the last three rules is unacceptable. The rules define the meaning of negation in terms of *falsum*, and the meaning of *falsum* in terms of negation: the rule for negation elimination is also a rule for *falsum* introduction, and the rule for negation introduction is also a rule for *falsum* elimination. Using these

---

19. Nonetheless, together with *ex contradictione quodlibet* as the elimination rule for negation, a system can be formulated in which deductions normalise.

three rules leads to a circular dependence between the meanings of negation and *falsum*. Dummett argues that there should be no such circular dependence between the meanings of the logical constants (Dummett 1993, 257). Hence this is not a viable option for defining the meaning of negation by rules of inference in the Dummettian framework.

We are left with Dummett's option of defining $\neg A$ as $A \supset \bot$, where $\bot$ is governed solely by *ex falso quodlibet* and by its usual introduction and elimination rules. Different arguments can be given why *ex falso quodlibet* satisfies the criterion of harmony. Prawitz argues that it is harmonious with the empty introduction rule (Prawitz 1979, 35). Dummett likens *falsum* to a universal quantifier over atomic formulas (Dummett 1993, 295). The details need not concern us here. What is important is that the negation so defined is intuitionist, not classical. Thus intuitionist logic is the correct logic according to Dummett's proof-theoretic justification of deduction.

Following this line of argument, classical negation can be excluded, as it requires the rule *consequentia mirabilis*:

$$\frac{\displaystyle \frac{\overline{\neg A}^{\,i}}{\begin{array}{c}\Xi\\ \bot\end{array}}}{A}\,i$$

As already discussed, this rule cannot be used to define the meaning of negation in terms of *falsum*, as it cannot count as defining the meaning of *falsum* independently of negation. It presupposes negation, which may occur in discharged premises. *Consequentia mirabilis* could only count as defining the meaning of *falsum* in terms of negation. But Dummett argues that the meaning of negation has to be defined in terms of *falsum*. Hence, once more, employing *consequentia mirabilis* produces a circular dependence of the meanings of *falsum* and negation. Dummett concludes that intuitionist negation does and classical negation does not satisfy the criteria of the proof-theoretic justification of deduction.[20]

It follows that the negation of a sentence is always semantically more complex than the sentence itself. $A \supset \bot$ is in general semantically more complex than A on anyone's account, as at least for some atomic propositions, a speaker can understand A without understanding $\supset$. Hence

---

20. The discussion of the previous section contains the material necessary to exclude other ways of extending intuitionist logic to classical logic in a similar way.

Dummett is in a position to claim that Geach's view that a sentences and its negation are of equal semantic complexity must be rejected in favour of a view on which A is less complex than $\neg A$.

4.2 The classical plan of attack

The rules governing classical negation do not fit the restrictions that Dummett's and Prawitz' proof-theoretic justification of deduction imposes on the form of self-justifying rules of inference. The classicist may, however, question whether this gives good reasons for rejecting classical logic. Dummett's and Prawitz' argument relies on the assumption that the meaning of negation can be defined by rules of inference. In the next section, I shall argue that this assumption is incorrect. *Ex falso quodlibet* fails to confer its intended meaning on $\bot$. Hence the meaning of intuitionist negation cannot be defined by rules of inference either. But then nothing can be amiss if the same is true for classical negation and its rules.

If rules of inference are not understood as completely determining the meaning of the constant they govern, then there is no rationale for requiring that they satisfy the demands of the proof-theoretic justification of deduction. For instance, as rules of inference alone are not sufficient to define the meanings of the connectives F and P with intended interpretation 'It will be the case that' and 'It has been the case that', tense logic is not subject to the proof-theoretic justification of deduction. The fact that the rules and axioms for P and F do not satisfy its requirements in no way shows that there is something wrong with them. The rules governing a connective are subject to the restrictions that the proof-theoretic justification of deduction imposes on the form of rules of inference if and only if the meaning of the connective is to be defined purely by the rules of inference governing it. Thus the fact that classical negation rules do not satisfy the criteria of the proof-theoretic justification of deduction is insignificant when it comes to reasons for rejecting classical logic.

4.2.1 The meaning of negation cannot be defined by rules of inference

Consider what $\bot$ is intended to be: a sentence that is false under any circumstances. Reading off its meaning from the rules governing it, the result should be that we cannot but say that $\bot$ is false. Although this characterisation of $\bot$ appeals to semantics, it does not violate the intended semantic neutrality of the proof-theoretic justification of deduction. It is legitimate to appeal to our semantic knowledge in order to see whether we have reconstructed it correctly in a given meaning-theory. Looking from the outside, as it were, at someone using ⊥ according to the rule *ex falso quodlibet*, are we bound to say that he cannot mean anything but a false sentence with it? The requirement that no semantic assumptions enter the theory is fulfled in this case, as no such assumptions enter the rule *ex falso quodlibet*. The question is: does it do the job it is supposed to do?

I think not. The intuitive content of *ex falso quodlibet* may be explained as follows: it says about ⊥ something like 'If you say this, you might as well say anything'. ⊥ is intended to be the ultimate unacceptable sentence, because everything follows from it. But what is it that makes a sentence from which everything follows unacceptable? It is that we assume that there are some sentences which are false.[21] If 'anything' covered only true sentences, there is nothing absurd in a sentence that entails that you may as well say anything. But it is a contingent feature of language that some sentences are false. Nothing prevents the atomic sentences of the language of intuitionist logic from all being true, and in that case every sentence, atomic and complex, would be true. Under these conditions, ⊥ could be true. So *ex falso quodlibet* does not give the intended meaning to ⊥, as it is not the case that we cannot but say that it is false.[22] More precisely, if every atomic sentence of the language was true, then far from ⊥ having to be false, it might be true. If all we know about ⊥ is what *ex falso quodlibet* tells us, then for all we know ⊥ might be equivalent to the conjunction of all atomic sentences, and if they are all true, ⊥ would be true.[23] So there are circumstances under which ⊥ may be true, namely if all atomic sentences are true. So we are under no necessity to say that ⊥ is always false.[24]

---

21. Some philosophers might prefer the view that what is unacceptable about a sentence from which everything follows is that there is no such thing. As they won't accept Dummett's and Prawitz' views on how negation should be defined, we may exclude them from consideration.

22. In section 4.3.2 I argue that the lack of an introduction rule for ⊥ does not remedy this.

23. Dummett acknowledges the possibility of all atomic sentences of a language being true (Dummett 1993, 295). He also appears to countenance that complex sentences not containing negation can be logically true (Dummett 1993, 266). This suggests that maybe he envisages a solution along the lines of section 4.3.1 below, which, however, I shall show not to be workable.

24. This argument occurred to me several years ago. I had to discover that other people found it as well, in particular (Hand 1999). Milne makes the related point that any deduction of a negated sentence relies on negated premises or discharged hypotheses. He concludes that 'it is quite impossible for ¬-introduction to determine the meaning of ¬' (Milne 1994, 61). The argument has its full force, however, only if it is placed in the larger context in which it is produced here, because of the multi-layered nature of Dummett's argument against classical logic: even if the meaning of negation cannot be defined proof-theoretically, some response is needed

Ironically, the reason why the definition of the meaning of *falsum* via *ex falso quodlibet* is appealing is that implicitly it appeals to *different models* for the language. This smuggles in semantic assumptions. It assumes that ⊥ is interpreted as having the same truth-value under every interpretation. This is not something that could be got from the rule. It is an assumption about how the semantics of ⊥ is to be given, which is external to the rule and thus illegitimate in the present context: it would not be the rule alone that determines the meaning of ⊥.

Dummett faces a predicament. He argues that from the proof-theoretic perspective, the meaning of negation needs to be given in terms of ⊥. But for *ex falso quodlibet* to confer on ⊥ the meaning of a constantly false sentence, the 'anything' it stands for would need to cover some formulas containing negation, it being understood that A and $\neg A$ are never true together. So the meaning of ⊥ can only be given with reference to negation. This is circular.[25]

The classicist and the intuitionist are consequently in exactly the same situation with respect to their attempts at defining the meaning of negation proof-theoretically. Dummett claims that the use of *consequentia mirabilis*, the rule specifying the use of both *falsum* and negation in classical logic, engenders a circular dependence of meaning between negation and *falsum*, and it now has been established that the same can be said about intuitionist negation.[26]

I conclude that the meaning of negation cannot be defined purely proof-theoretically by rules of inference in the Dummettian framework. Consequently, if Dummett's proposal is that the meaning of a logical constant can be defined purely in terms of its use in deductive arguments

---

to the molecularity challenge. Incidentally, an analogous argument purporting to show that the intended meaning of ⊤ cannot be given by rules of inference has a rather less clear status. ⊤ has only an introduction rule, but no elimination rule, which species that it follows from every sentence. In a language which contains just ⊤ and atomic sentences, where all atomic sentences are false, ⊤ could be false. But any language can be extended to contain logical constants defined by rules of inference, in particular ⊃. Then there will always be true sentences in a language.

25. A designated absurdity like 0 = 1 instead of ⊥ makes no difference. It is hard to see how *ex absurdo quodlibet* might then be justified, if not because one already accepts *ex contradictione quodlibet* and uses 0 = 1 as inducing a contradiction, which is again circular. This works at best in special contexts like arithmetic where 0 = 1 does the job it is supposed to do due to the axioms of arithmetic, hence not purely due to rules of inference governing it. In section 4.3.1, I argue that a more mundane absurdity like 'a is red and green all over' does not do the trick either.

26. In **R** there is even less of a chance of defining the meaning of negation in terms of rules of inference: the relevant *falsum* constant **f** is not governed by any rules which are not also negation rules. At the very outset it must be assumed that we either understand relevant *falsum* or negation.

if and only if this use can be characterised by harmonious introduction and elimination rules, then he is wrong. Even though in intuitionist logic *falsum* is governed by harmonious rules, its meaning cannot be defined by these rules. Only the *only if* part holds. There are logical constants the meaning of which cannot be determined by the harmonious rules governing them.[27]

4.2.2 *Consequences for the theory of meaning*

The ingenious idea of Dummett's proof-theoretic justification of deduction can be characterised as follows. On the basis of the assumption that speakers can follow rules of inference and grasp a concept of truth, which is neutral in the sense that none of its logical properties are specified prior to an investigation into which logic is the correct one, the proof-theoretic justification of deduction defines the meanings of the logical constants, amongst them negation. The resulting rules for negation then settle the question which properties truth has. As these rules are intuitionist, the principle of bivalence is not fullfilled. Only *positive* notions are appealed to as the primitive notions of the theory of meaning, *viz.* truth, assertion, affirmation, but not *negative* ones, like falsity, denial and negation. Assuming both notions of truth and falsity as basic would prejudge issues between classicists and intuitionists, because each will assume these notions to stand in their favourite logical relations to each other. The classicist will assume notions of truth and falsity that satisfy the principle of bivalence, whereas the intuitionist will assume notions which don't. The proof-theoretic justification of deduction was designed to settle the debate between classicists and intuitionists on neutral grounds. The choice of primitives, truth and rules of inference, rather than truth and falsity, was supposed to ensure this neutrality.[28]

---

27. According to Gentzen, *ex falso quodlibet* has a *Sonderstellung* amongst the rules of inference: 'it does not belong to one of the logical symbols, but to the propositional symbol [⊥]' (Gentzen 1934, 189). Adopting this view cannot help Dummett and Prawitz, as the question remains where our understanding of ⊥ comes from.

28. The point can also be made by noting that, if truth and falsity are chosen as primitives, intuitionists and classicists need to say something about the relation between the two notions, e.g. that nothing can be both true and false. This relies on using negation in the metalanguage, as in 'If *A* is true, *A* is not false'. Arguably, the negation of the object language will then mirror the properties of negation in the metalanguage, and hence, because classicists and intuitionists will each use their favourite logic in the metalanguage, neither has given a neutral justification of logical laws.

The definition of the meaning of negation in terms of rules of inference fails. The attempt turns out to be circular. In proof-theory, just as we assume that the meanings of the atomic sentences of the language are given, we need to assume that the meanings of their negations are given, too. The main insight to be drawn from the present discussion is that *positive* as well as *negative* primitive notions are needed in the theory of meaning. The argument of the last section once more suggests Geach's view on negation, so that speakers' understanding of the meaning of negation is an additional primitive of the proof-theoretic justification of deduction.

If the meaning of negation cannot be given purely by rules of inference, its rules are of a different nature from the rules of those connectives where this is possible. In the latter case, we can give the rules governing a constant from scratch, so to speak: a speaker can be taught the concept by being taught the rules. Just as we must assume prior understanding of 'It will be the case that' and 'It used to be the case that' in formalising tense logic, as learning the rules and axioms of tense logic are not sufficient to impart this understanding on a speaker, we must assume that we possess the concept of negation prior to formalisation. Laying down rules of inference for negation builds on this understanding. Although the rules tell us something about the intended interpretation of the symbol, they cannot impart understanding of the concept formalised.[29]

4.3 *Three counter-arguments refuted*

A Dummettian who'd rather not assume an understanding of the meaning of negation as a primitive might attempt to modify the proof-theoretic justification of deduction as a response to the argument that the meaning of negation cannot be defined by rules of inference. In the following, I shall discuss three accounts that attempt to do so. I shall show that each of them, though possibly interesting in their own rights, fails to satisfy Dummettian strictures imposed on the proof-theoretic justification of deduction.

---

29. Milne may have something similar in mind, when he says that its rules 'characterise' negation (Milne 1994, 85). Restricted to negation, it is in line with the views of Arthur Prior, who argued that inferential relations and truth-tables are devices of 'putting people on the track of the meaning of a word' and 'can help us in this way to fix the meaning of a word': they are a piece of 'informal pedagogy' (Prior 1964, 160 & 164).

4.3.1 *The nature of atomic sentences*

One retort is to claim that Dummett's atomic sentences cannot be atomic in the sense of Wittgenstein's *Tractatus* (Wittgenstein 2003, 6.3751) and of formal logic, where they are independent of each other and no conjunction of atomic formulas is always false and no disjunction of them is always true. If $\bot$ is to do its job, amongst Dummett's atomic sentences there must be some that *exclude* each other and cannot be true together. Surely this is supported by ordinary language, where there are such mutually exclusive atomic sentences, say 'a is red' and 'a is green'. Then *falsum* could not but be false, as it entails mutually exclusive atomic sentences.[30]

At a first glance, this looks like a natural way out. However, it defeats its purpose. To adopt this approach is in fact to admit that the proof-theoretic definition of the meanings of the logical constants fails in the case of negation, as it is obviously not a purely proof-theoretic definition. Proof-theory is not concerned with what the atomic sentences of a language are like; any collection will do. That the amendment is spurious is also seen if we consider that if it was adopted it would be a matter of luck that we have a language with a decent negation. Couldn't it be that a language is as the *Tractatus* claims it to be and lacks mutually exclusive sentences? Thus even if it is granted that some languages may contain mutually exclusive sentences, there are circumstances under which $\bot$ need not be false, namely if a language fails to have this property. Far from solving any problems for Dummett and Prawitz, it should evoke Frege's comments on Mill's gingerbread arithmetic: 'wie gut doch, dass nicht Alles in der Welt niet- und nagelfest ist' (Frege 1990, 9); how convenient indeed that our language is such that it contains the sentences it does in fact contain, as otherwise we couldn't do logic properly.

Rhetoric aside, one might of course try to advance arguments that for some reason or other there must always be true as well as false sentences in a language, or that a language could not be as Wittgenstein would have it in the *Tractatus*, or at least that any language could always be extended in such a way as to contain mutually exclusive sentences, or that the meanings of sentences are propositions and there are true ones and false ones amongst them. I have already mentioned that according to Dummett, using truth and falsity both as primitive fails to meet his requirements. Quite gener-

---

30. This was my initial reaction when I found the argument of section 4.2.1. (Tennant 1999) also proposes it in reply to (Hand 1999).

ally, the amendments just suggested cannot ensure that the meaning of negation can be defined by rules of inference. They all leave proof-theory and rely on assumptions external to it. One might object that if molecularity as a principle motivated by the philosophy of language may enter the proof-theoretic justification of deduction, then why not also let other theses shape the theory, like the ones just mentioned, which maybe could also be argued for in the philosophy of language? This question misses the point that there is a crucial difference between molecularity and these further theses. Molecularity is a principle that enters the *form* of the rules. Contrary to that, these further theses affect their *content*. But the content was precisely what was to be determined *exclusively* by the rules. Hence no matter how well these theses might be established in the philosophy of language, making them an essential part of the proof-theoretic justification of deduction has the effect of letting the theory collapse.

Although the 'amendments' to Dummett's theory mentioned in this section may very well be interesting new approaches to defining the meaning of negation, they are in fact not amendments at all, but incompatible with Dummett's approach.

4.3.2 *Falsity and assertibility*

Another attempt is to argue that the intended meaning of $\bot$ is captured by the rules governing it, as $\bot$ is governed by an elimination rule only and no introduction rule. So it has no grounds for its assertion. Hence there are no conditions under which it may be correctly asserted, hence under which it is true. So it can only be false.[31]

First, this a *non sequitur* and still does not guarantee that $\bot$ is indeed always false. Although being always false is a *sufficient* condition for something not to have grounds for its assertion, this is not *necessary*. That something has no grounds that warrant its assertion does not entail that it is false. It could be that we cannot assert it because we cannot put ourselves in a position to assert all the premises it relies on. No one would claim that the conclusion of the ω-rule is always false.

Secondly, the attempt is of no use in the present context. An intuitionist could be perfectly happy with the claim that *ex falso quodlibet* determines the meaning of $\bot$ completely. On an intuitionist understanding of falsity, if it can be proved that something has no warrant, then it is false, and nothing

---

31. *Cf.* (Prawitz 1979) and (Read 2000, 139).

is easier than showing that this holds for $\bot$, as it has no introduction rule. The problem is that this reasoning presupposes the anti-realist's notion of truth, explained in terms of assertibility. That something is unassertible entails that it is false only given the anti-realist notion of truth. Hence if this line of thought were used in the explanation of the meaning of *falsum*, it would certainly not be true of intuitionist logic that 'its logical constants can be understood, and its logical laws acknowledged, without appeal to any semantic theory and with only a very general meaning-theoretical background.' (Dummett 1993, 300) An analogous way would obviously be open to the classicist, using *his* preferred notion of truth. No explanation of the meaning of $\bot$ that satisfies the requirements of the proof-theoretic justification of deduction in being semantically neutral is forthcoming.[32]

4.3.3 *Empty succedents*

Maybe the argument put forward to show that the meaning of negation is not definable in Dummett's way asks for the impossible, given the framework he chose for formalising logic: if an arbitrary B is said to follow from $\bot$, fair enough, $\bot$ might be true. But isn't this shortcoming easily rectified if, instead of B, we allow an empty space to occur?[33] To explain validity in the modified natural deduction framework, we adopt a suitable modification of an explanation of the validity in sequent calculi, where multiple and empty conclusions are allowed: a sequent $\Gamma : \Delta$ is valid if, whenever all of Γ are true, some of Δ are true. Surely then, if from $\bot$ only emptiness follows, it must be false.

No doubt, this reasoning towards an always false $\bot$ is unassailable. The only problem with it is that it has the cart before the horse in the context

---

32. Appeal to warrants is not in itself biased towards intuitionism. Read describes himself as giving an account of the meanings of the logical constants in terms of what warrants an assertion of a complex formula with the constant as main connective (Read 2000, 130). He proposes infinitary rules for the quantiers (*ibid.*, 136). If Read's notion of a warrant was an anti-realist one, it would follow that we can assert the negation of every universally quantified sentence. The assumption that $\forall xFx$ is assertible would entail a sentence which is never assertible, namely that we have checked an infinite number of sentences Ft_j, understood as an *actual, completed* infinity, for otherwise we could not proceed to draw the conclusion. Analogously for existentially quantified formulas. Read's notion of a warrant needs to be understood in a realist sense: for some warrantedly assertible sentences it is not within our powers to obtain those warrants. Read does not give a *neutral* justification of classical logic, but a rather unsurprising one on the basis of a realist notion of warrant, which is hard to distinguish from a realist notion of truth. Similar remarks apply to Hacking, who also recommends infinitary quantifier rules (Hacking 1979, 313).

33. As suggested in (Tennant 1999).

of the proof-theoretic justification of deduction. The explanation of the validity of sequents is a semantic one: an inference is valid if it is truth preserving. On Dummett's view of the matter, the proof-theoretic justification of deduction must forswear the use of semantic notions in defining validity and instead define it in proof-theoretic terms: harmonious rules are self-justifying and valid purely by virtue of their form. That these rules are truth-preserving is a consequence of harmoniousness. The explanation of the validity of sequents does not fit with Dummett's outlook and, indeed, makes the proof-theoretic justification of deduction a rather idle pursuit. Without it, there is again no guarantee that interpretations of the language on which *falsum* is true are excluded, even if empty spaces are employed.

5. *Conclusion*

To sum up the dialectics of this paper, the argument against *tertium non datur* was intended as an argument that appeals only to very general considerations about the form a Dummettian theory of meaning has to take. It assumes that there is a difference in semantic complexity between $A \vee \neg A$ and $\neg(A \vee \neg A)$. The classicist can respond by pointing out that this assumption is unwarranted, as the same conceptual resources are required to understand each of them. The argument against rules yielding classical negation is an attempt to improve upon the situation by making a further assumption: that there are negation-free sentences B the double negation of which is true. Then the rules for classical negation license uses of B not otherwise licensed, which results in a circular dependence of meaning, contradicting Dummett's requirement of molecularity. This argument assumes that $\neg B$ is semantically more complex than B. A classicist can counter by arguing that a sentence and its negation should count as being of the same semantic complexity, as their understanding requires the same conceptual resources on the part of the speaker. Adopting Geach's view of negation, A and $\neg A$ occupy the same position in the partial ordering dependence of meaning imposes on the expressions of a language in a molecular theory of meaning. The Dummettian response is an attempt to establish that the negation of a sentence is indeed semantically more complex than the sentence itself. The argument is based on the proof-theoretic justification of deduction and aims to achieve two things: first, $\neg A$ needs to be defined as $A \supset \bot$, which is undeniably more complex than A, and secondly, only intuitionist but not classical negation is governed by rules of inference satisfying the requirements imposed. The classicist response is to point out that the meaning of ⊥ cannot be defined by rules of inference in the Dummettian framework, and hence the meaning of negation cannot so be defined either. Thus the fact that the rules for classical negation do not fulfil the requirements of the proof-theoretic justification of deduction does not warrant its rejection. I conclude that Dummett has not formulated a fair objection to classical logic on the basis of considerations about the form a theory of meaning has to take.

The classicist responses to the Dummettian arguments do not challenge the meaning-theoretical assumptions of Dummett's programme, molecularity and the principle that meaning is use. They do not appeal to any assumptions which are specifically classical, such as a realist notion of truth. The responses prejudge no issues between classicists and intuitionists. No charge of circularity can be put against them.

The strength of the classicist line of defence is also its weakness. Nothing in the proposed answers to the Dummettian challenges suggests that classical logic has to be preferred over intuitionist logic. An intuitionist can accept all the assumptions made in the classicist responses. The Dummettian programme, modied in the light of the fact that the meaning of negation cannot be defined proof-theoretically by adopting negation as a primitive notion along Geach's lines, is logically rather more neutral than Dummett had thought his original project to be: it is compatible with both classical and intuitionist logic. I shall leave the question what conclusions to draw from this for another occasion.

6. *Appendix*

I argued that Geach's view on negation suggests itself as a supplement to the proof-theoretic justification of deduction, so that negation is an additional primitive on the same par as affirmation. There is a promising alternative approach that shares the insight that positive as well as negative primitives are needed. Huw Price has suggested that sense should be specified in terms of two primitive speech acts, assertion and denial, where negation can be defined in terms of them.[34] The difference is important enough: Price suggests to double pragmatic primitives, I suggest to double semantic ones.

---

34. See (Price 1983), (Price 1990), (Price 2015). (Smiley 1996) and (Humberstone 2000) follow up some of Price's ideas. (Rumtt 2000) calls the position *bilateralism* and provides a formal development of a logic for assertion and denial.

I omitted bilateralism in the main part of this paper, as it is reasonably far removed from Dummett's original framework and deserves consideration on its own rights. At the request of several readers, I add this appendix to say a few words about Price's and Rumfitt's approach. I discuss them in detail in two separate papers. To avoid giving away too much of their content, I'll restrict myself to summarising results established there. There is, however, an independent point to this appendix, namely to indicate that it is preferable to leave the 'unilateral' framework of proof-theoretic semantics as it is and adopt the two primitives affirmation and negation rather than change the framework to one in which the primitives are assertion and denial. Even if we accept that negation is a primitive, that doesn't mean we can't say anything interesting about it, so towards the end I also say a few words about how I envisage an account of negation to proceed.

Most philosophers accept Frege's view that there is no need to posit a primitive force of denial (Frege 1918, 153). We cannot understand certain inferences, such as those where the minor premise is rejected and the major premise is a conditional with a negated antecedent, in terms of a force of denial, as a speech act cannot be embedded into a conditional. We need negation as a sentential operator. But then denial is redundant, as we can define it in terms of negation and assertion. Price's and Rumfitt's accounts are more complicated than the unilateral account. It seems as if bilateralism only succeeds in introducing needless complexities.

Bilateralism and unilateralism aren't, however, equivalent theories, according to Price and Rumfitt. They aim to meet a well-known Dummettian challenge: to provide a framework for a theory of meaning that justifies classical logic but does not suffer from the shortcomings Dummett claims such an approach must face, by ensuring that it provides for a notion of sense intelligible to the kind of speakers that we are. Even Dummett and his most ardent followers, I think, agree that it would be preferable if classical logic were the justified one. Price and Rumfitt claim that bilateralism succeeds in justifying classical logic, whereas unilateralism does not. If that is correct, then the complexities of bilateralism are justified, as they result in establishing a theoretical *desideratum*, namely the justification of classical logic.

In two papers on bilateralism, one on Price and one on Rumfitt, I argue that each approach fails to justify classical logic as the unique logic. Price's account, ironically, works better for intuitionist logic. In a similar vein, it is possible to formulate an intuitionist bilateral logic in Rumfitt's framework in which the rules are harmonious, just as they are for classical logic.

Thus the complexities bilateralism introduces into the debate fail to serve their purpose of justifying classical logic as the unique correct logic. This means that the unilateral approach of the current paper is to be preferred over the bilateral approach on methodological grounds.

In the paper on Price, I regiment Price's account by formulating axioms that capture the concepts Price employs in his argument that bilateralism justifies classical logic. Price proposes a pragmatic account of belief in terms of the differences they make to speakers' actions. My formalisation shows a certain amount of redundancy in the concepts Price employs. It turns out that the axioms entail consequences about the notion of making a difference that Price can't accept: if classical logic is correct, the notion is either vacuous or highly problematic. As my axiomatisation follows Price's wording very closely, it cannot be argued that the result merely shows my axiomatisation to be wrong. I show how a very small modification—adding a 'not' at a place in an axiom characterising disbelief where one would expect one anyway—insures that the notion of making a difference regains its interest. The theory is then, however, best seen as intuitionist, and classical logic cannot be established on the basis of it. My axiomatisation uses all the resources Price provides, so to get classical logic, Price needs to extend his account. This may of course be possible, and I consider Price's options, but all this establishes is that both alternatives are possible, not what Price had intended to show, namely that only the classical version is justified.

Rumfitt poses the intuitionist a challenge: to provide a bilateral account of intuitionist logic in which the rules of the system are in harmony. Rumfitt demands of the intuitionist a specification of what in general follows from the denied negation of a formula that is harmonious with the introduction rule for denied negations. Classicists and intuitionists agree that the denied negation of a formula follows from its assertion. The harmonious elimination rule, according to Rumtt, is that the asserted formula follows from its denied negation. This is only acceptable to the classicist, not the intuitionist. I show how to formulate different rules that are also harmonious, but result in an intuitionist bilateral logic. Thus Rumfitt's challenge is met. This is not the place to go into the formal details, but harmonious rules for an intuitionist bilateral logic can be formulated by making a fuller use than Rumfitt himself does of the possibilities offered by the formal framework of bilateral logics.

As neither Price's nor Rumfitt's approach lends itself exclusively to the classicist, but in each case an intuitionist alternative can be formulated, for methodological reasons—that a simpler theory is to be preferred over an equivalent more complex one—it follows that the unilateral approach proposed in this paper comes out as superior to its bilateral rivals.

Rumfitt's formalism also faces an independent problem of how to interpret deductions carried out in it. In Rumfitt's bilateral logic, the premises, discharged assumptions and conclusions are supposed to be understood as asserted or denied formulas. Rumfitt accepts that speech acts cannot be embedded in other speech acts. Thus, the formulas in Rumfitt's system cannot be understood as being prefixed by 'It is assertible that' and 'It is deniable that', as these are sentential operators and can be embedded. Rumfitt's bilateral formalism faces a fundamental conceptual problem: what does it mean to assume an assertion or a denial in a deduction? Arguably, this makes no sense, as it is plausible that making an assumption is a speech act.

Even if the meaning of negation cannot be defined by rules of inference within proof-theoretic semantics, we can still give an account of it. This is the aim of another paper of mine. For the purposes of this appendix, an indication of the general idea should suffice. Just as the meaning of a predicate, say 'is red', cannot be given purely by rules of inference, but the colour red has to figure in how its meaning is determined, the meaning of 'not' has to be given by reference to something other than rules of inference. Inferential relations may play an important role in determining the meaning of an expression even if that meaning cannot be completely determined by rules of inference. The predicate 'is red' gets its meaning from the inferential relations is stands in with other colour terms and what it refers to, the colour red. The structure colours exhibit together validates inferences such as that what is red is not green. Negation enters the understanding of concepts that exhibit complex inferential structures, like the colour words, and thus cannot be understood without a grasp of that structure. Certain metaphysical consideration may enter the Geachean account, but that is unsurprising: the relation between affirmation and negation is connected to facts about the world. It is the point where metaphysics enters logic. If the meaning of negation cannot be defined within proof-theoretic semantics, this means that it loses the purity that Dummett envisaged it to have. It is important, however, to stay as neutral as possible when it comes to the question of whether classical or intuitionist negation is the correct one. Another question to be addressed in my paper is whether, on the basis of my Geachean account of negation, Dummett's complaints about multiple conclusion logics can be shown to be unfounded: this gives a smooth and elegant route to justifying classical logic. The paper aims to show how, building on Geach's ideas, a viable account of negation can be given that fills the gap in proof-theoretic semantics identied in the present paper, but nonetheless stays true to its spirit.

References

Belnap, Nuel 1962: "Tonk, Plonk and Plink". *Analysis* 22, 130–134.
Dummett, Michael 1981: *Frege. Philosophy of Language*. 2nd edition London: Duckworth.
— 1991: *The Seas of Language*. Oxford: Oxford University Press.
— 1993: *The Logical Basis of Metaphysics*. Cambridge, Mass.: Harvard University Press.
Frege, Gottlob 1918: "Die Verneinung. Eine logische Untersuchung". *Beiträge zur Philosophie des deutschen Idealismus* 1, 148–157.
— 1990: *Die Grundlagen der Arithmetic. Eine logisch-mathematische Untersuchung über den Begriff der Zahl*. Hildesheim, Zürich, New York: Olms.
— 1998: *Die Grundgesetze der Arithmetik*. I/II. Hildesheim, Zürich, New York: Olms.
Geach, Peter T. 1971: *Mental Acts*. London: Routledge.
— 1972: "The Law of Excluded Middle". In: *Logic Matters*. Oxford: Blackwell, 74–87.
Gentzen, Gerhard 1934: "Untersuchungen über das logische Schließen". *Mathematische Zeitschrift* 39, 176–210, 405–431.
— 1936: "Die Widerspruchsfreiheit der reinen Zahlentheorie". *Mathematische Annalen* 112, 493–565.
Hacking, Ian 1979: "What Is Logic?" *Journal of Philosophy* 76, 285–319.
Hand, Michael 1999: "Anti-Realism and Falsity". In: Dov Gabbay & Heinrich Wansing (Eds.), *What is Negation?* Dordrecht: Kluwer, 185–198.
Humberstone, Lloyd 2000: "The Revival of Rejective Negation". *Journal of Philosophical Logic* 29, 331–381.
Kürbis, Nils 2012: "How Fundamental Is the Fundamental Assumption?" *Teorema* 31, 5–19.
— 2013: "Proof-Theoretic Semantics, a Problem with Negation and Prospects for Modality". *The Journal of Philosophical Logic* (forthcoming in print, DOI: 10.1007/s10992-013-9310-6).
Miller, Alexander 2002: "What Is the Manifestation Argument?" *Pacific Philosophical Quarterly* 83, 352–383.

Miller, Alexander 2003: "What Is the Acquisition Argument?" In: Alex Barber (Ed.), *Epistemology of Language*. Oxford University Press, 459–495.

Milne, Peter 1994: "Classical Harmony: Rules of Inference and the Meanings of the Logical Constants". *Synthese* 100, 49–94.

Prawitz, Dag 1965: *Natural Deduction*. Stockholm, Göteborg, Uppsala: Almqvist and Wiksell.

— 1979: "Proofs and the Meaning and Completeness of the Logical Constants". In: Jaakko Hintikka, Ilkka Niiniluoto & Esa Saarinen (Eds.), *Essays on Mathematical and Philosophical Logic*. Dordrecht: Reidel, 25–40.

Price, Huw 1983: "Sense, Assertion, Dummett and Denial". *Mind* 92, 161–173.

— 1990: "Why 'Not'?" Mind 99, 221–238.

— 2015: "'Not' Again". http://prce.hu/w/preprints/NotAgain.pdf (accessed 18/07/2015).

Prior, Arthur 1961: "The Runabout Inference Ticket". *Analysis* 21, 38–39.

— 1964: "Conjunction and Contonktion Revisited". *Analysis* 24, 191–195.

Read, Stephen 2000: "Harmony and Autonomy in Classical Logic". *Journal of Philosophical Logic* 29, 123–154.

Rumfitt, Ian 2000: ""Yes" and "No"". *Mind* 109, 781–823.

Smiley, Timothy 1996: "Rejection". *Analysis* 56, 1–9.

Tennant, Neil 1999: "Negation, Absurdity and Contrariety". In: Dov Gabbay & Heinrich Wansing (Eds.), *What is Negation?* Dordrecht: Kluwer, 199–222.

Wittgenstein, Ludwig 2003: *Tractatus Logic-Philosophicus*. Frankfurt am Main: Suhrkamp.

PLAIN PARTICULARS

Ernâni MAGALHÃES
Fishers, Indiana

Abstract
Are concrete objects in some sense made up of the properties they exemplify? A distinguished tradition holds they are. I begin by defending the distinction: there is a real and not just semantic distinction between asserting and denying that concrete objects have their properties as parts. I then argue in favor of the view that concrete objects are not made up of their parts. First, this view has less ontological baggage than its opponent. Next, the supposed advantages of the alternative view—its superiority in understanding persistence, exemplification, or the possibility of diverse duplicates—dissipate under analysis.

Keywords: Concrete object, properties, bare particulars, metaphysics, persistence, indiscernibility

Are particular objects in some sense made up of the properties they exemplify? According to a distinguished tradition, concrete particulars[1] are composites, bundles, or states of affairs that have their properties as constituents, elements, or parts (Sider 2006, 387; Benovsky 2008; Allaire 1963; Alston 1954; Russell 1948, 97; van Inwagen 2011). For now, let's set aside possible differences between composition, constituency, elementhood, and other allied relations and refer to properties on this conception as constituents of their particulars. And let us call a theory according to which particulars have their properties as constituents a Constituency Theory.[2] Opponents of the Constituency Theory deny that particulars

---

1. That is, tables, chairs, horses, electrons, and so on.
2. To use Peter van Inwagen's (2011, 390) terminology, Constituency Theorists advocate a constituent ontology. That is, they hold that concrete particulars have ontological structure insofar as there are non-particular objects that have quasi-mereological relations to them. Constituency Theorists as I understand them, unlike van Inwagen's constituent ontologists, hold that the properties that constitute particulars are exemplified by those particulars. The constituent

have their properties as constituents. Mostly for ease of reference, I will call the denial of Constituency Theory Plain Particularism.[3] In addition to its denial of the Constituency Thesis, I will associate Plain Particularism with a few other theses about particulars and their relationship to their properties. These theses will be explained momentarily.

Both Constituency Theorists and Plain Particularists of course agree that particulars are usually complex in an ordinary sense: cars are made up of wheels and engines, human beings have arms and legs, trees have branches and leaves, and so on. But advocates of the Constituency Thesis believe that particulars are complex along an additional dimension. They are made up of properties. According to Plain Particularists, particulars are simple along this qualitative dimension.

Both Constituency Theorists and Plain Particularists also agree that particulars exemplify properties,[4] change, that there could be distinct indiscernible particulars, and that there cannot be particulars that don't exemplify properties. They disagree in that Constituency Theorists believe they can explain what it is for a particular to exemplify a property, to change, to be distinct yet indiscernible, and why it is that particulars must exemplify properties. Plain Particularists deny these explanations. In fact, Plain Particularists deny the need for any explanation for these phenomena. While a Plain Particularist will agree that there are many informative things to be said about particulars as an ontological category, on the view, particulars are not ontologically analyzable in the way suggested by Constituency Theory. Instead, particulars should be admitted as an ultimate, not further analyzable, ontological category.

In this paper I will argue that Plain Particularism is superior to a specific version of Constituency Theory. According to one kind of Constituency Theory, the bundle theory, particulars are bundles of properties (Benovsky

---

ontologist is neutral on this point, although each of the constituent ontologies van Inwagen discusses holds the same.

3. Van Inwagen's label for the rejection of constituency theory, "relational ontology," is unfortunate because it suggests some relation is at the core of the view. Because the main items at issue in the debate about whether properties constitute particulars are particulars and their properties, the natural inference is that on a relational ontology particulars exemplify properties by having some relation to them. E. J. Lowe (2012, 234) understands the view this way. But as van Inwagen himself recognizes, it is better to think of exemplification not as a relation, but as unanalyzable.

4. It seems to me that nothing I say in this paper precludes a Plain Particularist from rejecting the existence of properties. He might paraphrase apparent reference to properties in some nominalist way. The Plain Particularist writing this paper happens to think the paraphrasing project will not be successful.

2008).⁵ The properties in the bundle make up a particular because they are compresent.⁶ A particular object exemplifies a property because that property is a constituent of the bundle in which it is compresent with some other properties. According to the substratum theory, the version of Constituency Theory that will be the concern of this paper,⁷ particulars are constituted not only by the properties they exemplify but by a substratum. A particular object exemplifies a property because that property is a constituent that inheres in the substratum along with whatever other properties also inhere in the same substratum.

Plain Particularists and substratum theorists agree on the truth of certain propositions, but they disagree on their status. While the Plain Particularist holds that these propositions are not susceptible to further analysis or informative metaphysical reduction, the substratum theorist proposes a set of further propositions that are alleged to analyze or provide the metaphysical basis for the phenomena described by the target propositions. The agreed upon propositions are these:

(Exemplification) Particulars exemplify properties.
(The Rejection of Unqualified Particulars) Necessarily, particulars exemplify properties.⁸
(Change) Particulars change.
(Distinct Indiscernibles) Possibly, there are distinct indiscernible particulars.

---

5. By "properties" I mean "non-relational qualities." I use the term neutrally between trope and universals theory. I consider below Sider's (2006, 387) argument that substratum theorists should think of properties as mereologically composing the particulars they make up.

6. I assume this is the traditional bundle conception where there really are bundles of properties which cannot merely be identified with the properties that constitute "them" à la van Cleve's (1985) third version of the bundle theory.

7. It is unclear to what extent the argument of this paper could be extended to bundle theories. For example, bundle theory may be less theoretically complex than substratum theory, and therefore at less of a deficit to Plain Particularism from the get-go. Also, bundle theorists sometimes deny what I take to be common ground in this discussion, that indiscernibles may be distinct. A referee also wonders whether it matters if properties are universals or tropes. Substrata typically—but not always (Martin 1980)—bring along universals rather than tropes.

8. More exactly, necessarily, if particulars exist then they exemplify properties. Armstrong (1979, 113) calls this the rejection of bare particulars. Since substratum theorists accept bare particulars, aka, substrata, this would be a very misleading term for the view. The thesis rejects the idea that there are any ordinary particulars that do not exemplify properties; it does not reject the idea that there are nonqualitative constituents of ordinary particulars, i.e., substrata.

Plain Particularists and substratum theorists agree on the conjunction of: Exemplification, The Rejection of Unqualified Particulars, Change, and Distinct Indiscernibles. Substratum theorists go on to assert certain propositions regarding ontological structure that are alleged to provide the metaphysical basis of those four.

It would be nice if a theory of the nature of particulars could be tested by considering possible or actual particulars that do not satisfy the theory or possible or actual entities that satisfy the theory but are not particulars. But the concept of a concrete particular seems so general as to make the method of counterexample hopeless. I, at least, am unable to think of more or less concrete scenarios where something satisfies the substratum theory but is not intuitively a concrete particular or where something is intuitively a concrete particular but does not satisfy the theory. Instead I will compare the two theories on their capacity to handle various dialectical pressures. I will argue that (1) substratum theory begins at a substantial deficit compared with Plain Particularism because of the additional and mysterious entities and relations it postulates; and (2) substratum theory does not make up for this deficit by providing superior accounts of the four phenomena. In fact, the explanations substratum theorists offer do no more than restate the phenomena. Before coming to the main argument, I begin with some previous discussions of Constituency Theory and substratum theory.

1. *Van Inwagen's arguments against Constituency Theory*

In "Relational vs. Constituent Ontologies," Peter van Inwagen presents some arguments against the Constituency Theory (van Inwagen 2011, 393–398). These arguments are directed both at substratum and bundle theories. I show in this section that these arguments do not really tell against Constituency Theory and therefore that plenty of work remains to be done in showing the flaws of that view. As he acknowledges, van Inwagen's "principal reason" for rejecting Constituency Theory is no more than the confession that he does not understand non-mereological constituency (van Inwagen 2011, 393). Absent some reason for thinking that the concepts the Constituency Theorist appeals to cannot be understood, van Inwagen's ignorance may as likely be due to a fault in him as to a fault in the theory. Nonetheless, his extended confession includes some comments that may be construed as something more than the mere expression of van Inwagen's ignorance. Whether these comments are intended as an argument or not, it is interesting to see what plausibility they have so considered.

Van Inwagen notes that according to the Constituency Theorist the mass of an electron—say, $9.11 \times 10 \exp -31$ kg—may be among its constituents (van Inwagen 2011, 394). One can divide this entity by six, multiply it by some other quantity, and so on. But van Inwagen finds it nonsense to suppose that something to which one can apply arithmetical operations could be a constituent of a physical thing like an electron.

Why should it be that if arithmetical operations apply to something then that something cannot be a constituent of a physical thing? Van Inwagen doesn't say and it's hard to think of some premises for this assertion that don't assume the falsehood of Constituency Theory. One might say that things to which arithmetical operations apply are not spatio-temporal, but then a Constituency Theorist will disagree and hold that at least some things to which arithmetical operations apply are spatio-temporal (Armstrong 1988, Swoyer 1987). Or one might say that things to which arithmetical operations apply cannot be physical and any constituents of an electron must be physical. But then the Constituency Theorist will surely deny that the constituents of an electron must be physical and even non-Constituency Theorists may want to hold that arithmetical operations apply to physical things (Yi 1998, 103).

Van Inwagen's second official reason for rejecting Constituency Theory is that Constituency Theorists appeal to a confused methodology or notion of explanation to arrive at their theory of particulars (van Inwagen 2011, 396-398). Taking their model from scientists, Constituency Theorists seek to explain, in some problematic sense of the term, certain phenomena concerning particulars such as that they may exemplify properties and that two of them may share a property.

First, at best this is a flaw not with Constituency Theory but rather with an argument for it. The Constituency Theorist is alleged to arrive at his view by following a certain method. This method is said to be flawed. From this obviously it doesn't follow that the view is flawed. A reason to reject Constituency Theory must be a problem with the theory that results, not with the path that leads one there.

Second, there is little to be said for assuming that the Constituency Theorist partakes in this allegedly problematic notion of quasi-scientific explanation. Why not suppose that the Constituency Theorist is engaged in the entirely benign and mundane philosophical enterprise of seeking to arrive at a theory that illuminates something in much the way that one may seek to better understand knowledge, fiction,[9] or properties themselves? So in much the way that one tries to understand the fictional world so that we may say all we want to say about Don Quixote, so we may try to understand particulars so that we may say all we want to say about them.

Finally, it appears that there is a notion of explanation that is neither what is used in science nor fundamentally problematic. One may explain why water freezes but one may also explain why the number two is even. Putting forth some propositions about what two is and what being even is from which it follows in an illuminating way that the number two is even seems a perfectly acceptable example of explanation, even if it is not quite what is done in offering a scientific explanation. The sort of explanation the Constituency Theorist may be supposed to put forth is of just this sort: he proposes some propositions about the nature of particulars from which it is alleged to follow in an illuminating way that Exemplification, Change, Distinct Indiscernibles, and so on.

In sum, van Inwagen's criticisms leave a great deal to be done in comparing the merits of Constituency Theory and Plain Particularism.

2. *Is there really a distinction between substratum theory and Plain Particularism?*

An initial challenge to the claim that Plain Particularism is superior to substratum theory is the thought that the Plain Particularist's particular is just the substratum theorist's substratum or thin particular. Perhaps then Plain Particularism and substratum theory are just different ways of saying the same thing. There are a number of reasons to think this is not the case. First, the substratum, unlike the Plain Particularist's particular, is conceived to be a constituent of a concrete particular. The Plain Particularist's particular is not a constituent of a concrete particular but rather itself a concrete particular. Second, even where this notion of constituency has not been assumed, the notion of a substratum has been different from a plain particular. David Armstrong, for example, claims that sometimes when we are thinking about particulars we have in mind thin particulars (Armstrong 1979, 114). A thin particular, he says in a popular formulation,

---

9. Van Inwagen (1977, 302) explains the ontological categories that creatures of fiction belong to.

is "a thing taken in abstraction from all its properties."¹⁰ The thought seems to be that the thin particular is what remains after all its properties have been set aside. This may strike some as suspiciously similar to the plain particular, which does not include any of its properties as constituents.

But this abstractionist conception of the thin particular is not the Plain Particularist's conception of a particular. A particular, Plainly understood, is not "a thing taken in abstraction from all its properties." To "take[]" a thing "in abstraction" from its properties is to perform a certain mental operation. The fact that something is a particular, however, has nothing to do with the mental attitude we take toward it. Furthermore, one can "take[]" something "in abstraction" from its properties even if there is no such item as the thing without the properties. One might take or consider, for example, the number two in abstraction from the property of being even. But there is no such thing as the number two without the property of being even.

In addition to defining this notion of a particular in terms of a certain mental performance, the definition has the further defect of singling out the wrong thing at the end of the operation. Suppose there is something that corresponds to one's taking a thing in abstraction from all its properties.¹¹ What would that thing be like? The thing—the thin particular or allegedly the Plain Particularist's particular—would not have any of the particular's properties.¹² But the Plain Particularist wants no part of saying that a particular is something that has none of that particular's properties. The Plain Particularist's particular is precisely that which exemplifies the particular's properties.

---

10. In his (1997, 115), Armstrong says the thin particular is "the particular apart from its properties."

11. Giberman (2012, 308) says the bare particular "is 'what is left' when we mentally abstract away all of a material object's properties." If something "corresponds" to that conception, he says, it is a bare particular. So on this notion I conceive of something as bare when I conceive the material object without any of its properties. There are two ways in which something might "correspond" to this concept. First, I might conceive X in a certain way, and X actually exists even if not in that way. That is likely not the intended sense, since on this definition every (existing) conceived material object would be bare. Or, the thing might correspond to the conception in the sense that it exists in the way conceived. So something would correspond to my conception in this second sense if it were the material object I am conceiving but didn't have any of the material object's properties (or any others, presumably). But that won't work either—no one thinks there are material objects that have no properties.

12. What properties, if any, the resulting thing, the thin particular, would have is the subject of some dispute (Sider 2006, Bailey 2012). Because I take no position on this debate, I will speak of substrata as instantiating or being associated with the properties exemplified by the particular.

In a similar spirit, Theodore Sider has argued that the dispute between "those who think that a particular contains its universals as parts and those who think that it does not" is "merely verbal" (Sider 2006, 388).[13] Since substratum theorists hold that properties are constituents of their particulars and Plain Particularists deny this, it would appear that Sider is challenging the distinction I have drawn. However, it is unclear what exactly is the target of Sider's argument, and to the extent his argument can be construed as directed toward this distinction it is unsuccessful.

Sider characterizes this dispute about whether properties are parts of particulars as being "among" substratum theorists (Sider 2006, 388). Unfortunately, Sider also characterizes substratum theory as holding that particulars are mereological composites made up of both properties and substrata (aka, "thin particulars"):

> [T]he bundle theory says that a particular is exhaustively composed of . . . its universals. The substratum theory, on the other hand, denies this. Take a particular, and mereologically subtract away its universals. Is anything left? According to the bundle theory, no. But according to the substratum theory, something is indeed left. Call this remaining something a "thin particular". (Sider 2006, 387)

Substratum theory, therefore, holds that a particular is a mereological composite of all of its universals plus the remaining non-universal, the thin particular. Since substratum theorists by Sider's own definition hold that particulars are composites of properties and substrata, there can be no dispute among them about whether particulars have their properties as parts.

But let us see whether Sider's argument against the substantiality of the dispute about whether particulars have properties as parts can be understood simply as concerned with those who affirm and those who deny that properties are parts or constituents of particulars. Sider proceeds to argue as follows:

> Call the fusion of a particular and its universals a "thick particular." The mereological difference between a thick particular and its universals is . . . a thin particular. All substratum theorists agree that thin and thick particulars both exist. Thick particulars contain their universals as parts, thin particulars do not. Whether *particulars* have their universals as parts then depends on

---

13. Nothing hinges on Sider's assumption that properties are universals or that constituency is parthood here.

the nonissue of whether one means thick or thin particulars by 'particulars'. (Sider 2006, 388)

So supposedly the question whether a particular is constituted by its properties reduces to whether we should think of "particulars" as meaning the same as "thick particulars" or "thin particulars."

First, it is far from clear why deciding between "thick particular" and "thin particular" as the semantic content of "particular" is a trivial matter. To discover the meaning of "particular" would appear to be a significant achievement, especially discovering whether by definition to be a particular something must have its properties as constituents. "Particular" is hardly a term of art to be stipulatively defined by metaphysicians.[14]

Second, the apparent triviality of the dispute seems to be merely an artifact of unduly restricted terminology. A thick particular, by definition, is a composite of a particular and its universals. A thin particular, by definition, is something that includes a particular but not its universals. But why should we restrict ourselves to only these two conceptions of a particular? One can readily define the notion of a medium particular: something that includes a particular and which may or may not include its universals. That is, the notion is neutral on the inclusion of universals as parts. With these definitions, it is a perfectly substantive question whether particulars are thick, thin, or medium.

Sider presents a different version of the argument in his 1995 (367f.). He argues that any dispute about whether properties are parts of particulars is "pointless" on the assumption that properties are spatio-temporally located where their particulars are. I believe a Plain Particularist should be open to the possibility that properties are spatio-temporal, though I will not expand on that conception here. So I want to see the prospects of the argument on this assumption. This time Sider defines thick and thin particulars more helpfully as follows. The thick particular is, e.g., the composite of an electron along with its properties. A thin particular is, e.g., the mereological difference between the electron and its properties. Sider argues that on these assumptions

[t]hick and thin particulars would have identical locations, and anything we want to say about particulars can be said just as easily whether they are thick

---

14. Although "particular" does not actually get much use in its relevant sense in ordinary parlance, allied terms implicated in this debate do. If it is a matter of stipulative decision whether "particular" means "thick" or "thin particular" it must similarly be a matter of stipulative decision whether "tiger" means "thick tiger" or "thin tiger," "electron" means "thick electron" or "thin electron," and so on. These terms can hardly be claimed to be susceptible of stipulative definition.

or thin. For example, we can speak of the relation of "thin instantiation" which holds between thin particulars and universals; but we can speak just as easily about the relation of "thick instantiation", which holds between a thick particular and the universals the corresponding thin particular thinly instantiates. Surely, our talk of electrons, people, etc. would simply be indeterminate between talk of thick particulars and talk of thin ones, and so there would be no sense in arguing over whether particulars are thick or thin.

As Sider makes explicit in his 2006, the argument assumes that there are both thick and thin particulars. Plain Particularists believe that there are particulars that exemplify properties. One of the benefits of the view is that they need not believe that there are also entities that include as constituents both particulars and properties. So a Plain Particularist may well want to deny that there are both thick particulars and thin particulars. Indeed, the assumption that there are both thin and thick particulars may well reflect the notion that this dispute again is understood as internal to the substratum theory. Within the substratum theory, of course it is plausible to assume that everyone agrees that there are both substrata and complexes made up of substrata plus properties.

It does appear to be true that assuming spatio-temporal properties, thick and thin particulars would have the same locations. The rest of the passage, which expresses two arguments for the insubstantiality of the dispute about the Constituency Thesis, is not so successful. First, there is a very abbreviated argument for the conclusion that "anything we want to say about particulars can be said just as easily whether they are thick or thin" (Sider 1995, 372). Second, there is a very abbreviated argument involving the claim that our particular talk is "indeterminate" as between thick and thin particulars.

As to the first argument, the rest of this paper will be concerned with various areas in which it makes a difference whether or not properties are construed as constituents of particulars. The gist of Sider's example here begins by noting that we want to say that particulars instantiate properties. The Plain Particularist can understand instantiation in terms of a "relation" between a particular and a property. The substratum theorist can "just as easily" understand instantiation as a relation "between a thick particular and the universals the corresponding thin particular thinly instantiates." However, the non-equivalence of the two accounts can be seen by noticing that the two theories posit different "relations" and different "relata" to explain property-having. The substratum theorist's account of particular instantiation requires not only an instantiation connection between the substratum and the property but also a constituency relation between the thick particular and the property element. Also, instantiation connects a particular and a property on the Plain Particular theory. The substratum theorist's instantiation connects a thick particular, a thin particular, and a property. It is difficult to see how these could be different ways of saying the same thing.

As to the second argument, I am not sure whether our talk about particulars is indeterminate as between thick and thin particulars. Before being convinced that it is, I would need to see something more than just a bare assertion. Furthermore, even if our talk about particulars is indeterminate between the two conceptions, the metaphysical question would remain seemingly unaffected. Consider those entities which are particulars; are they constituted by properties or not? Even if the answer is not settled by the meaning of "particular," there may be other metaphysical considerations that support one or another conception.

Before moving on to a discussion of these metaphysical considerations, it is worth pausing to note a difficulty with Sider's purely compositional version of substratum theory. This view holds that concrete particulars are not states of affairs or otherwise bundles of their constituents. Instead, they are made up of their qualitative and substratum elements in just the same mereological way that human beings are made up of their cells. In the substratum theory as developed by Sider, a concrete particular is a composite of the relevant properties and the substratum.

Consider that concrete particulars can be decomposed to different levels. My arms, legs, torso, etc., compose me. Also, at a different level of decomposition, my cells compose me. Similarly, since composition is the same in ontological structure as in physical structure, I can be decomposed into my properties and substratum as well as my cells. If the Xs compose Z and the Ys compose Z then it follows that there must be something, A, that overlaps one (or more) of the Xs and overlaps one (or more) of the Ys.[15] But this principle does not seem to apply if ontological structure is just another level of mereological decomposition. A ball is composed of red, round, mass M, etc. It is also composed of certain electrons. But there

---

15. This follows from van Inwagen's (1987, 22f.) classic definition of composition. If the Xs compose Z then Z is the sum of the Xs; and if the Ys compose Z then Z is the sum of the Ys. So, every part of Z must overlap at least one of the Xs, and every part of Z must overlap at least one of the Ys. Since Z is a sum, it must have parts. And each of these parts will overlap at least one X and at least one Y.

is no guarantee that there is something that is a part of both one of red, round, mass M, etc. and those electrons.[16]

3. *At the starting line*

In this section I spell out the ontological commitments of Plain Particularism and substratum theory. I show that at the starting line—that is, pending an examination of the phenomena to follow—substratum theory is less credible than Plain Particularism because it posits more entities—including relations, connections, or whatever— and because we have little if any independent grasp on these entities.

Plain Particularists posit concrete particulars, their properties, and some connection between them in virtue of which the former exemplify the latter. They also postulate certain axioms about particulars. Particulars exemplify properties. Particulars cannot exist without exemplifying properties. They change. And there are or could be distinct yet indiscernible particulars. Substratum theorists also posit concrete particulars, their properties, and some connection between them in virtue of which the former exemplify the latter. While the story offered by the Plain Particularist is just what I have said, the substratum theorist's is much more complicated. In explaining property exemplification, substratum theorists posit a constituency relation that connects the property and the concrete particular so that the property is a constituent of the particular. Substratum theorists also posit substrata, which are the non-qualitative core of particulars. This substratum supports the properties of the particular. It also serves to individuate different particulars (Armstrong 1979, Moreland 1998, Bergmann 1967). Substratum theorists also postulate certain axioms. Substrata support properties.[17]

---

16. One could find a guarantee on certain assumptions. Suppose properties are abundant in the sense that there is a property for every meaningful predicate. And suppose that, just as with concrete particulars, when a property exemplifies a property, the property exemplified is a part of the property doing the exemplifying. So red exemplifies the property of being self-identical insofar as being self-identical is a part of a composite made up of certain properties (and perhaps a substratum). Then, because red is self-identical and my cells are all self-identical, there will be something, the property of being self-identical, that is a part both of red and of my cells. But note that the reason for the overlap between red, round, etc., and my cells has nothing to do with their both composing me. Being self-identical overlaps both red, round, etc. and my cells just because it overlaps everything.

17. Moreland (1998, 258): "it is a primitive fact that properties are tied to them [bare particulars] and this does not need to be grounded in some further capacity or property within them. In analytic ontology, one eventually comes to primitives … [T]here is no need to ground

Necessarily, substrata do not exist without supporting some properties. Substrata may exist at distinct times even though they support incompatible properties at those times. And possibly, substrata may be distinct even though they support all the same properties.

At the starting line—that is, absent further arguments—it seems Plain Particularism is significantly more reasonable than substratum theory. This is because substratum theory requires belief in all sorts of entities that Plain Particularism does not require. Between two theories, the one that postulates more entities and relations is a priori less likely to be true. In addition, many if not all of the substratum theory's extra entities are mysterious posits with which we are familiar only through their roles in substratum theory.[18] I am unaware of any efforts to explain the notions of substratum, inherence, support, and constituency in ways that purport to make these entities comprehensible apart from the theory. The difficulty of appealing to notions that are entirely theoretical—that is, constructed—is that one's understanding of the concepts is exhausted by what has been explained. Any further questions one has about the entities, absent those features that are entailed by their asserted character, have no determinate answers. In other words, their nature seems to be invented to fit a purpose rather than discovered as with real entities. Even champions of the substratum have acknowledged the difficulty of accepting at the core of their theory of particulars an entity with which we are never acquainted (Allaire 1963, 2).

This advantage of Plain Particularism may be overcome after we leave the starting line and examine the particular phenomena that give rise to the substratum theorist's posits. Theoretically, if there were some advantages to substratum theory in some of these domains, one would need to weigh these against Plain Particularism's advantage in simplicity. This won't be necessary because, as I will argue, none of the phenomena to be examined support the substratum theorist's theoretical framework. The rest of this paper is devoted to considering whether the substratum theorist's account of Exemplification, The Rejection of Unqualified Particulars, Change, and Distinct Indiscernibles provide some reason to think that substratum theory is superior to Plain Particularism.

---

the inherence of properties in a bare particular by way of some further entity within it when we recognize that 'inhere in' is taken as 'tied to'."

18. This is not true in the case of constituency, which arguably occurs in other phenomena, although I also don't know of any illuminating explanation of this relation, either.

4. *Exemplification*

One desideratum of an acceptable theory of particulars is that it give some story of what happens when particulars exemplify properties. In this section, I consider the substratum theory's account of exemplification and compare it with Plain Particularism's. I argue that the substratum theory's account does not provide any reason to prefer it to Plain Particularism.

Just what is involved in a particular's exemplifying a property? According to the substratum theorist, two things are going on when a particular exemplifies a property. First, as J.P. Moreland and Timothy Pickavance put it, the property is "rooted within" the complex entity that includes the various property constituents (Moreland and Pickavance 2003). That is to say, the property is a constituent of the particular.[19] Second, the property must have the appropriate connection to the other constituents of the particular. The substratum theorist holds that the property must inhere in the substratum that is unique to that particular.[20]

What about the Plain Particularist's theory of exemplification? When a particular exemplifies a property, there is one thing, a particular, and a distinct thing, a property, and the one exemplifies the other. To be sure, this is not, and in no way claims to be, an analysis of exemplification.[21] But this is indeed an advantage of this view. It should be no surprise that exemplification would not be susceptible of analysis. If any phenomenon in all of philosophy has a good claim to be unanalyzable surely exemplification is it. To see the benefit of acquiescing in the ultimate character of exemplification, one need look no further than the inelegant complexity and ultimately unilluminating character of the substratum theorist's alternative.

Is it any improvement in our understanding of exemplification to say that when a particular exemplifies a property, there is a substratum entity within the particular in which the property inheres? To the extent one understands the substratum it is because of its resemblance to an ordinary particular. A substratum seems to have many of the properties of an ordi-

---

19. Bundle theorists also explain a particular's having properties in terms of the properties being constituents of the particular (Benovsky 2008, 176).
20. Alston (1954, 258) discusses "two senses of exemplification": when the pencil exemplifies yellow, that's inclusion (257); the relation between the substratum and universal is underlying (257).
21. van Inwagen (2011, 398) similarly denies that the exemplification of properties by concrete particulars is susceptible to further elucidation: "no set of statements … counts as an explanation of what it is for a particular to have a property."

nary particular: it seems to persist through time, to change, to have modal aspects. The substratum's supporting properties sounds a lot like what a particular does when it exemplifies properties. To the extent supporting a property is different from exemplification, no one really knows what sort of thing it is supposed to be. But to the extent supporting a property is just exemplifying it, the analysis of exemplification is caught in a tight circle. To further our understanding, an analysis of a phenomenon must appeal to other phenomena on which we have some grip. The substratum theorist's analysis of exemplification fails this elementary test.[22]

5. *The Rejection of Unqualified Particulars*

One of the major motivations for substratum theory is the sense that particulars are intimately connected with their properties. Surely a particular is intimately connected with its properties if the properties are actually contained in the particular. But what is the precise content of the notion that particulars are intimately connected with their properties? A popular thought is that particulars are intimately connected with properties insofar as particulars cannot exist unless they have properties. There is surely something questionable about the idea of a particular that lacks properties. Let us call the doctrine that particulars cannot exist without exemplifying properties the Rejection of Unqualified Particulars. In this section I argue that the Plain Particularist is in no worse a position than the substratum theorist in trying to justify the Rejection of Unqualified Particulars.

Substratum theorists have an initially appealing explanation for why particulars cannot exist without properties. According to substratum theory, a particular must be constituted by properties. That is its nature. A particular's existence involves there being something that is constituted by properties in the right way. Being constituted by properties in the right way means having property elements that are the properties of the particular. So of course on the substratum theory, a particular could not exist unless it exemplified properties.

And initially it looks as if Plain Particularism is inferior on this score. According to the view, a particular is wholly diverse from its properties. As Armstrong (1979, 76) puts it in a related context, particulars and proper-

---

22. Moreland (1998, 260) asserts that substrata come "with properties tied to them in a primitive way ungrounded in capacities or properties within" them.

ties "stand apart" from each other. If particulars and their properties are "separate," how can there be a necessary bond between them such as that required by the fact that particulars must have properties?

The substratum theory's explanation of the Rejection of Unqualified Particulars in fact masks a problem similar to that of the connection between particulars and their properties. Because of this the substratum theory is no better than Plain Particularism in accounting for the Rejection of Unqualified Particulars. Particulars require properties, on this view, because particulars are constituted by properties that inhere in substrata. So substrata play the crucial role of connecting to properties to make qualified particulars. But this story is of little use if substrata themselves can exist without having or supporting properties. It is surely no more plausible to think that substrata can exist without properties than it is to suppose that particulars exist without properties. And according to Moreland (1998, 257), substrata "do not exist unless they possess properties." So what metaphysical story can be told to explain why substrata must have properties? One can explain this situation by maintaining that it is in the nature of substrata to have properties. But this explanation is no better than what is available to the Plain Particularist, who may just as well say that it is in the nature of particulars to exemplify properties.

Moreland (1998) suggests a couple of reasons to suppose that substrata must come attached to properties. First (p. 261), perhaps there are "transcendental properties" that are "truly predicable of all entities whatsoever." Since such properties qualify everything, they would also have to qualify substrata, and therefore substrata could not exist without supporting at least those properties. Second, Moreland hints at a "general theory of existence that requires entities to have properties in order to exist" (p. 261). If everything must have properties in order to exist, so must substrata.

It should be obvious that both of these lines are available to Plain Particularists. They can with equal plausibility say that there are transcendental properties that are necessarily exemplified by all things and that existence requires the exemplification of properties.

6. *Change*

Particulars change. They have properties at one time that they lack at others. Can this fact about particulars be illuminated further? Does the supposed illumination offered by substratum theory constitute an improvement over the Plain Particularist's primitivist[23] account? Is there something in the nature of change that tends to support the substratum theory over Plain Particularism?

The problem of change is the problem of temporary intrinsics. How can one account for the fact that a particular may be F at T1 and not be F at T2? The substratum theory explains this by holding that a substratum can be connected to F at T1 and not be connected to F at T2.[24] It seems in order for genuine change to be possible, there needs to be some common element in the persisting object that survives whatever qualitative change it undergoes. For the substratum theorist, a particular can persist through change because there is a substratum that stays within the complex of properties and remains the same even as properties come in and out. According to Benovsky (2008, 179), the substratum theorist will say that when change occurs, there is a "substratum that remains the same over different times, and this guarantees me that the individual, while changing its properties, is the same individual."

The Plain Particularist, again, does not purport to identify an element that is common in the persisting individual from one time to the other. Apart from possible positions regarding the dispute between endurantism and other such theories, the Plain Particularist does not have anything informative to say by way of explaining how a particular persists through time.

Again, substratum theory turns out not to improve our understanding of the original phenomenon. On this view, a concrete particular can survive change because it has in it a substratum that survives change. In order to work, this account must hold that a substratum can only ever exist in one concrete particular. In other words, if a substratum is in particular P at T1, and the substratum is in some particular at T2, then the T2 particular is P. But this is not all the substratum needs to do. The existence of the particular at T1 and T2 doesn't seem enough to explain change. The element that guarantees the survival of the particular from T1 to T2 should also be that which underlies the changing properties. The substratum plays

---

23. In saying that change is primitive for a Plain Particularist, I don't mean to deny the possibility that the Plain Particularist will have some preference for endurantism over perdurantism, say. Whether persisting particulars are "wholly present" at each time when they exist or are rather space-time worms remains a live question even if Plain Particularism is true.

24. Some advocates of what I call substratum theory do not accept this conception of change. Generally, advocates of bare or thin particulars tend to hold that particulars persist by being composites of temporary stages (Armstrong 1979).

this special role in connecting to the particular's changing properties. The substratum supports the changing properties of the particular. A concrete particular, P, can survive change from being F at T1 to being not-F at T2 because it has a substratum in it at both times that supports F at T1 and supports not-F at T2.

This is little more than the original problem repeated. To the extent it is mysterious how a particular object can have incompatible properties at different times, it is at least as mysterious how a substratum can support incompatible properties at different times. On this suggested theory, there is a substratum that exists at T1 and supports F and exists at T2 and supports not-F. How can that be? Supporting incompatible properties at different times seems no easier to swallow without further explanation than exemplifying incompatible properties at different times. Because the substratum account of change does not improve our understanding of the phenomenon, it presents no reason to accept the constituent analysis that comes with it.

7. *Distinct Indiscernibles*

Another phenomenon that has traditionally motivated certain metaphysical conceptions of particulars and undermined others is the problem of the identity of indiscernibles. It seems possible that concrete particulars X and Y should have all the same properties and yet be distinct. What does it say about the nature of particulars that there can be distinct indiscernibles?[25] Does the possibility of distinct indiscernibles tend to support substratum theory over Plain Particularism? Again, I will argue that the substratum theorist's account of distinct indiscernibles is no improvement on the Plain Particularist's.

According to substratum theory, indiscernible particulars X and Y are nonetheless distinct because the substratum of X, X*, is distinct from the substratum of Y, Y*. Indiscernible particulars may be distinct because each particular has its own unique substratum. Necessarily, if X and Y are distinct particulars then the substratum of X must be distinct from the substratum of Y.

---

25. Black (1952) is the classic presentation. Mertz (2001, 48) puts the problem this way: "The problem of individuation is the problem of how we are to account for the *unrepeatability* of an entity when absolutely all of its characteristics ... are repeatable." Inevitably, some philosophers deny that there could be distinct indiscernibles (O'Leary-Hawthorne 1995).

What account of the phenomenon of distinct indiscernibles can the Plain Particularist give? The Plain Particularist, again, does not attempt to provide an explanation of the phenomenon. He takes as an axiom of his theory of particulars, that, possibly, there may be distinct particulars that have all the same properties. While substratum theory appears to do more than acquiesce in the phenomenon, by actually offering a theory of the phenomenon, in fact the theory does little more than restate the phenomenon it purports to explain.

The substratum theorist supposes that each particular has its own unique substratum. So X has X* and Y has Y*, and X* and Y* are distinct. Notice that X* and Y* support the same properties. What has happened here? The substratum theorist has invented a category of entity to account for the possibility of distinct indiscernibles. And then he has said that those entities can be distinct yet support all the same properties. It is surely no less mysterious how substrata can be distinct yet support the same properties than it is that concrete particulars can be distinct yet exemplify the same properties.

Some substratum theorists hold that X* and Y* exemplify properties, and thus the same properties, but some hold that these substrata do not exemplify but support the same properties.[26] So if the substratum theorist holds that X* and Y* do not exemplify properties then they are not distinct indiscernibles in the sense that X and Y are distinct indiscernibles. X and Y are distinct indiscernibles in the sense that they exemplify all the same properties; on this version of substratum theory, X* and Y* are only indiscernible in that they support all the same properties.

But even if supporting a property is different from exemplifying the property, as I have argued, to the extent we understand the phenomenon, it is on analogy with exemplifying a property. Thus it is mysterious how distinct substrata can support the same properties to the exact same degree that it is mysterious how distinct concrete particulars can exemplify the same properties. Moreland (1998, 260) admits that the substratum theorist's explanation of the possibility of distinct indiscernible particulars bottoms out on the possibility of distinct substrata that support all the same properties. The substrata in indiscernible distinct particulars, he says, "are simples and, as a matter of primitive fact, they simply come individuated even if properties are necessarily tied to them." So it is a primitive fact that substrata "come individuated" and are not in need of any further

---

26. See Bailey (2012) and his references.

individuation. And this is so despite the fact that substrata must be tied to properties and possibly distinct ones are tied to the very same properties. In short, it is a brute fact that substrata may be distinct yet support the same properties.

Before finishing up I pause to examine a different argument for substratum theory in this same neighborhood. Moreland (1998, 251) identifies a "problem of individuation," explaining it by reference to two red, round spots with all the same "pure properties." A solution to the problem requires "offering an ontological assay of the situation so as to specify what it is that makes the two spots two particular, individual entities instead of one." Moreland goes on to sketch and defend an account that appeals to bare particulars, i.e., substrata.

If solving the problem of individuation in this sense were a desideratum of a plausible theory of particulars, then Plain Particularism would be in some trouble. But there is little reason to accept the problem so characterized. It is a remarkable phenomenon that two spots may share all their "pure properties"—presumably those not defined in terms of some particular object, e.g., being taller than Steve. But why should the problem require offering an ontological *assay*? Though the dictionary definition does not require this, the expression has widespread usage in the philosophical world among those who think concrete particular entities and other entities can be analyzed into their constituent qualitative and other elements (Bergmann 1967, Mertz 2001). And a Plain Particularist has some reason to suspect that "specify[ing] what it is that makes the two spots two … instead of one" will require identifying some further entities in the spots in virtue of which the spots are two and not one.[27] The sense of "specify" intended likely does not include the following story. The spots are two because, at least, they are different.[28] Why are they different? Here one may as well be up front in confessing that no illuminating explanation will be forthcoming. The spots just are different. This is not an analysis of their difference, but nothing has been said to motivate the notion that their difference requires analysis.

---

27. Interpreting and taking up Moreland's problem of individuation, Mertz (2001, 49) writes that to solve the problem "what are required are constituents of each of [the indiscernible particulars], and these constituents must be unrepeatable and thus serve to distinguish" the particulars.

28. Being different may not suffice for being two—the clay and the statue it makes up may be different yet one (Moyer 2006)—but that is surely not the problem Moreland has in mind.

8. Conclusion

Constituency Theory holds that properties are in the particulars they qualify. One version of this view, substratum theory, holds that in addition to the properties that constitute a particular, there is something non-qualitative—substratum, thin, or bare particular—that supports those properties or in which they inhere. Plain Particularism, on the other hand, holds that properties are not elements of the particulars they exemplify; instead, particulars are wholly distinct from their properties. I have argued that Plain Particularism is superior to substratum theory. First, I criticized some of van Inwagen's complaints about Constituency Theory. Then I showed that Plain Particularism is genuinely distinct from substratum theory, despite the arguments by Ted Sider to the contrary. I then argued that the phenomena that supposedly support substratum theory—change, the possibility of distinct indiscernibles, exemplification, and the impossibility of unqualified particulars—in fact present no reason to believe substratum theory at all. Since substratum theory—with its extra and mysterious entities—begins at a significant disadvantage vis-à-vis Plain Particularism, Plain Particularism is the better "theory" of particulars.[29]

Bibliography

Allaire, Edwin B. 1963: "Bare Particulars". *Philosophical Studies* 14, 1–8.

Alston, William 1954: "Particulars—Bare and Qualified". *Philosophy and Phenomenological Research* 15, 253–258.

Armstrong, David M. 1979. *Nominalism and Realism.* Volume 1 of *Universals and Scientific Realism.* Cambridge: Cambridge University Press.

— 1988: "Are Quantities Relations? A Reply to Bigelow and Pargetter". *Philosophical Studies* 54, 305–316.

— 1997: *A World of States of Affairs.* Cambridge: Cambridge University Press.

Bailey, Andrew 2012: "No Bare Particulars". *Philosophical Studies* 158, 31–41.

Benovsky, Jiri 2008: "The Bundle Theory and the Substratum Theory: Deadly Enemies or Twin Brothers?". *Philosophical Studies* 141, 175–190.

Bergmann, Gustav 1967: *Realism: A Critique of Brentano and Meinong.* Madison, WI: University of Wisconsin Press.

---

29. Thanks to Richard Fumerton, Nathan Oaklander, and an anonymous referee for this journal for their helpful comments.

Black, Max 1952: "The Identity of Indiscernibles". *Mind* 61, 152–164.

Giberman, Daniel 2012: "Against Zero-Dimensional Material Objects (and Other Bare Particulars)". *Philosophical Studies* 160, 305–321.

Lowe, E. J. 2012: "A Neo-Aristotelian Substance Ontology: Neither Relational nor Constituent". In: Tuomas Tahko (ed.), *Contemporary Aristotelian Metaphysics*. Cambridge: Cambridge University Press, 229–248.

Martin, C. B. 1980: "Substance Substantiated". *Australasian Journal of Philosophy* 58(1), 3–10.

Mertz, Donald W. 2001: "Individuation and Instance Ontology". *Australasian Journal of Philosophy* 79, 45–61.

Moreland, James P. 1998: "Theories of Individuation: A Reconsideration of Bare Particulars". *Pacific Philosophical Quarterly* 79, 251–263.

Moreland, J. P., & Pickavance, Timothy 2003: "Bare Particulars and Individuation". *Australasian Journal of Philosophy* 81, 1–13.

Moyer, Mark 2006: "Statues and Lumps: A Strange Coincidence". *Synthese* 148, 401–423.

O'Leary-Hawthorne, John 1995: "The Bundle Theory of Substance and the Identity of Indiscernibles". *Analysis* 55, 191–196.

Russell, Bertrand 1948: *An Enquiry into Meaning and Truth*. London: Allen and Unwin.

Sider, Theodore 1995: "Sparseness, Immanence and Naturalness". *Noûs* 29, 360–377.

— 2006: "'Bare Particulars'". *Philosophical Perspectives* 20, 387–397.

Swoyer, Chris 1987: "The Metaphysics of Measurement". In: John Forge (ed.), *Measurement, Realism and Objectivity*. Dordrecht: D. Reidel, 235–290.

Van Cleve, James 1985: "Three Versions of the Bundle Theory". *Philosophical Studies* 47, 95–107.

Van Inwagen, Peter 1977: "Creatures of Fiction". *American Philosophical Quarterly* 14, 299–308.

— 1987: "When Are Objects Parts?". *Philosophical Perspectives* 1, 21–47.

— 2011: "Relational vs. Constituent Ontologies". *Philosophical Perspectives* 25, 389–405.

Yi, Byeong-Uk 1998: "Numbers and Relations". *Erkenntnis* 49 (1), 93–113.

FREGE AND THE DESCRIPTION THEORY: AN ATTEMPT AT REHABILITATION

Ari MAUNU
University of Turku

Abstract

I question the received view that Frege advocates the description theory of proper names. First, I argue that the textual evidence for this view from Frege's writings is not conclusive. Secondly, I propose that the Fregean *Sinne* (of proper names) may be understood nondescriptionally in terms of symbolhood. Finally, I suggest that in the notorious passages where Frege is apparently supporting the description theory he is just indicating the potential problems with communication with proper names.

Keywords: Frege, Gottlob; sense and reference; description theory; proper names; definite descriptions; symbolhood.

1. Introduction

The very rarely questioned received view has it that Frege advocates the description theory of proper names, that is, that the contents, or *Sinne* in Frege's terminology,[1] of ordinary proper names coincide with the contents of some appropriate definite descriptions. The evidence for this received view appears to consist mainly in the notorious second footnote of "Über Sinn und Bedeutung" (1892), where Frege seems to identify the *Sinne* of proper names with those of definite descriptions.

My purpose in this paper is to question this received view. In Section 2, I bring up some counter-evidence from Frege's writings. In Section 3, I suggest an interpretation of Frege's notion of *Sinn*, according to which

---

1. I use Frege's German words *Sinn* (*Sinne* in plural), *Bedeutung, Gedanke, Begriff* instead of their usual translations *sense, reference* (or *meaning*), *thought, concept* in order to emphasize that Frege uses them as technical terms, as he tells us, with regard to '*Gedanke*', in his manuscript "Logik" (NS 147f. / PW 135–37, 1897).

Sinn is to be understood nondescriptionally in terms of symbolhood. Armed with this interpretation, I explain in Section 4 what I think Frege is up to in the mentioned footnote as well as in the relevant passage in "Der Gedanke" (1918).

2. *Evidence and Counter-Evidence*

Frege writes in the second footnote of "Über Sinn und Bedeutung" as follows (KS 144n / CP 158n):

> In the case of an actual proper name such as 'Aristotle' opinions as to the sense may differ. It might, for instance, be taken to be the following: the pupil of Plato and teacher of Alexander the Great. Anybody who does this will attach another sense to the sentence 'Aristotle was born in Stagira' than will a man who takes as the sense of the name: the teacher of Alexander the Great who was born in Stagira.

On the face of it, this footnote is not much of evidence if the Frege corpus is taken as a whole. Or, in any case, it is extraordinarily uncharitable to impose a view regarded as important on a major philosopher (practically) on the basis of a single footnote. Yes, there is also the Gustav Lauben passage in "Der Gedanke" (1918), where Frege might be taken to endorse the description theory—however, there is nothing in that passage (to be discussed in Section 4 below) that could be taken as an *explicit* endorsement.

Evidence for the claim that Frege was *not* a description theorist is readily available in Frege's writings. In "Logic in Mathematics" (NS 243 / PW 225, 1914) Frege writes:

> 'Copernicus' and 'the author of the heliocentric view of the planetary system' designate the same man, but have different *Sinne*; for the sentence 'Copernicus is Copernicus' and 'Copernicus is the author of the heliocentric view of the planetary system' do not express the same *Gedanke*.

If one wanted to propose a definite description as an "abbreviation" of the name 'Copernicus', wouldn't 'the author of the heliocentric view' be the first that comes to mind?[2]

---

2. Also, NS 208 / PW 192, 1906: "The sentence 'Mont Blanc is over 4000m high' does not express the same thought as the sentence 'The highest mountain in Europe is over 4000m high', although the proper name 'Mont Blanc' designates the same mountain as the expression

One popular argument—let's call it the *triviality argument*—against the description theory has been that if the name 'a' "abbreviated" the definite description 'the F' then "a is the F" (as well as "a is an F") should be just as trivial and necessary as "the F is the F" (see, for instance, Kripke 1980, 12f.), which is preposterous. The last quote from Frege shows that

(P1) Frege considered the triviality argument.

Given the simplicity of that argument, it is plausible that

(P2) Whoever endorses the description theory, hasn't considered the triviality argument.

The refutation of the received view concerning Frege's descriptionism follows logically from P1 and P2:

(C) Frege doesn't endorse the description theory.

Further, even in "Über Sinn und Bedeutung" itself (KS 153f. / CP 168f.) we find the following:[3] Frege considers both "The discoverer of the elliptic form of the planetary orbits died in misery" and "Kepler died in misery". Frege says that it would be a mistake to take the *Sinn* of the former to contain the *Gedanke* that there was somebody who discovered the elliptic form of the planetary orbits. Frege then gives to "Kepler died in misery" a respective treatment by saying that it would be a mistake to take its *Sinn* to contain the *Gedanke* that the name 'Kepler' designates something. There is no indication here that a proper name is to be treated as an "abbreviation" of a definite description and, in any case, there should be no need for a

---

'the highest mountain in Europe'." I am indebted to an anonymous referee of GPS for directing me to this passage.

Cf. also *Grundlagen* (Frege 1884) §57: "There is nothing contained in the name 'Columbus' about discovery or about America, even though it is the same man that we call Columbus and the discoverer of America." It must be admitted, however, that Frege had not made the distinction between *Sinn* and *Bedeutung* at the time he wrote the *Grundlagen*. On the other hand, there are some anticipations of the distinction in that book (see GL §§66-67), and it could even be argued that for Frege the introduction of *Sinn* means basically only a certain reclassification or specification: "When I wrote my *Grundlagen der Arithmetik*, I had not yet made the distinction between *Sinn* and *Bedeutung*; and so, under the expression 'a content of possible judgment', I was combining what I now designate by the distinctive words '*Gedanke*' and 'truth-value'" (KS 172/ CP 187, 1892).

3. Tapio Korte directed me to this passage (personal communication).

description theorist to make such a separate point about a proper name. This gives indirect counter-evidence to Frege's being a descriptionist.

Finally, Frege states, frequently and emphatically, that sentences such as "Caesar exists" don't have a *Sinn*. (This is due to the incongruence of levels: existence is, for Frege, a second-level *Begriff*, which cannot be applied to an object (*Gegenstand*).) But why should a committed description theorist be so adamant about this? If the name 'c' really amounts to the description 'the F', one need not be a Russell to realize that sentences such as "c exists"—i.e., semantically equivalently, "The F exists"—can be represented by means of the existential quantifier, as "$\exists x(Fx \:\&\: \forall y(Fy \rightarrow y=x))$".

In sum, I think it is fair to say that there isn't in Frege's writings conclusive evidence for the received view that he advocated the description theory.

3. *Sinne*

In *Naming and Necessity*, Kripke (1980, 7–10), considering

(1) Aristotle was fond of dogs,

dismisses the view "that the simple fact that two people [e.g., the Philosopher and Onassis] can have the same name refutes the rigidity thesis" (p. 7). This is fine, of course, but what is significant is that Kripke says things like: "I perforce assumed a particular reading for (1)" (p. 8); (1) is given a "fixed understanding" (p. 9); and (1) "must be taken to express a single proposition" (p. 9, italics removed).

To my mind it is precisely here where the *Sinn* is needed: this very "fixing of understanding" or "particular reading" of a pattern is to confer a *Sinn* to it. To "understand" that the pattern 'Aristotle' in (1) is *this* symbol and *not any other* symbol is to attach to it a "way of being given" (*Art des Gegebenseins*) of a certain object and not any other object—'Aristotle' in (1) has *this* interpretation (*Sinn*) and *not any other* interpretation (*Sinn*).[4] That is, to take (1)—a pattern such as the one displayed in (1)—to express a certain proposition (say, about the Philosopher) and not any other proposition (like the one about Onassis) is, among other things, to adopt a "fixed understanding" or "particular reading" of 'Aristotle' in (1); I suggest that

---

4. It is natural to hold that 'Aristotle' as the name of the Philosopher is semantically distinct from 'Aristotle' as the name of Onassis. See, for instance, Kripke 1980, 8; Evans 1982, 384; Kaplan 1989, 562; Bealer 2002, 100n34.

this amounts to attaching to this 'Aristotle' a way of being given a certain object, or, as we may also say, to use it with a certain content that is not exhausted by its mere reference. In successful communication, participants must *share* something, it must somehow be clear to them just *what* are the symbols used, and this, I suggest, amounts to their attaching the same *Sinn* to the patterns they use. A pattern is *sinnvoll* to us only as a symbol: this applies to proper names as well, and therefore *Sinne* are indispensable in semantics: even proper names (as symbols) do have content (= *Sinn*) besides reference (= *Bedeutung*). The mere reference cannot fulfill this role (cf. the popular direct reference view that "the content/meaning of a proper name is exhausted by its referent" (or that "proper names lack content/meaning")).

To illustrate, if a shower of meteorites happened to form a huge pattern 'Aristotle', visible from the Earth, on the surface of the Moon, this pattern wouldn't, obviously, carry any interpretation with it. (I don't mean that we couldn't know which Aristotle is meant but that no Aristotle is meant at all.) Imagine that some people would think that the shower cannot be accidental and that, therefore, it must be that God is trying in this manner to relate to us the importance of Aristotle the Philosopher. These people would thereby interpret this token of 'Aristotle' in a certain manner, "assume a particular reading" for it, use it as a symbol, attach a *Sinn* to it, take it as a pattern with a content. (And, therefore, the *Bedeutung* of this pattern, so taken, would be "determined" for these people.)

This interpretation of *Sinn* is consistent with the description theory: One view is that this ability to use proper names as symbols, or the sharing of their *Sinne* between speakers, is due to the contents of definite descriptions. However, the description theory is by no means forced on the account of the *Sinne* of proper names outlined above: it suffices to hold that these sharings (or *Sinne*) are due to whatever it is that enables us to communicate with symbols. To repeat, Frege's point is that something— the *Sinne*—must be shared in communication or in any use of symbols. For this, names need not be taken as descriptive.[5]

---

5. Michael Dummett (1973) has maintained that even though it is Frege's view that a name, in a use, can be descriptional, "there is nothing in what he says to warrant the conclusion that the sense of a proper name is always the sense of some complex description" (Dummett 1973, 97f.; see also Evans 1982, 18). Dummett continues: "All that is necessary, in order that the senses of two names which have the same referent should differ, is that we should have a different way of recognizing an object as the referent of each of the two names: there is no reason to suppose that the means by which we effect such a recognition should be expressible by means of a definite description or any other complex singular term" (*ibid.*, 98). Dummett's view is that

4. *Frege's Apparent Endorsement of the Description Theory*

In "Der Gedanke" Frege writes as follows (KS 349f. / CP 358f.):

> Suppose [...] that Herbert Garner knows that Dr. Gustav Lauben was born on 13 September, 1875 in N.N. and this is not true of anyone else; suppose, however, that he does not know where Dr. Lauben now lives nor indeed anything else about him. On the other hand, suppose Leo Peter does not know that Dr. Lauben was born on 13 September 1875, in N.N. Then as far as the proper name 'Dr. Gustav Lauben' is concerned, Herbert Garner and Leo Peter *do not speak the same language,* although they do in fact refer to the same man with this name; for *they do not know that they are doing so* [my emphases]. Therefore Herbert Garner does not associate the same thought with the sentence 'Dr. Gustav Lauben was wounded' as Leo Peter wants to express with it. [...]
>
> Accordingly, with a proper name, it is a matter of the way that the object so designated is presented. This may happen in different ways, and to every such way there corresponds a special sense of a sentence containing the proper name. The different thoughts thus obtained from the same sentences correspond in truth-value, of course; that is to say, if one is true then all are true, and if one is false than all are false. Nevertheless the difference must be recognized.

Frege doesn't advocate the description theory in this passage. Rather, he is making it clear how background knowledge may affect communication with proper names, even to the point that the speakers in a communication situation are in effect using distinct symbols, that is, attach distinct *Sinne* to what is in fact communally one and the same name.[6] In using a symbol that on the communal level is in fact a single symbol, speakers may be uncertain whether there are in fact two symbols at hand. Two speakers may even think that they are really using distinct symbols—this happens when they think that they are referring to distinct objects (or don't know that they are referring to the same object), as in Frege's just-quoted Gustav Lauben passage. According to Frege, in this case "as far as the proper

---

attaching a *Sinn* to a proper name is to associate a "criterion of identification" to that name (see, for instance, *ibid.,* 111). What I am suggesting, in contrast to Dummett, does not concern at all "a way of recognizing an object" or "a criterion of identification" but, rather, the fact that using a pattern with a "fixed understanding" amounts to regarding it as *sinnvoll.*

6. An equiform name with the same referent (in different uses) is here termed 'communally the same name'. (Strictly speaking, they should also have the same chain of communication, cf. Kripke 1980, 8n9.)

name 'Dr. Gustav Lauben' is concerned, Herbert Garner and Leo Peter do not speak the same language" and do not "associate the same thought with the sentence 'Dr. Gustav Lauben was wounded'", which proves that in Frege's view they indeed attach distinct *Sinne* to 'Dr Gustav Lauben' (surely, it is taken for granted in this example that they share *Sinne* with 'was' and 'wounded'). Of course, even a single speaker may take what is in fact (communally) a single symbol as two distinct ones (in different contexts), i.e., attach two different *Sinne* to an expression (an example of which is Kripke's (1979) Paderewski case).

My suggestion is that also in The Footnote in "Über Sinn und Bedeutung" Frege is indicating potential problems of communication in ordinary discourse—though, unfortunately, in a very quick-and-dirty manner. If speaker A knows about Aristotle only that he was the most prominent student of Plato and speaker B knows about the very same Aristotle only that he was the most famous teacher of Alexander (and both A and B use the name 'Aristotle'), then A and B do not, indeed, share a symbol (*Sinn*) in using 'Aristotle'—and one need not be a description theorist in advocating this view.

5. *Conclusions*

(i) There is in Frege's writings no conclusive evidence for the received view that he advocated the description theory.

(ii) To attach a *Sinn* to a "proper name pattern" is just to take this pattern as a particular symbol—the description theory is dispensable.

(iii) The Gustav Lauben passage in "Der Gedanke" and, arguably, also the notorious footnote in "Über Sinn und Bedeutung" are about, not the description theory but problems with communication with proper names.[7]

---

7. In writing this paper, I am deeply indebted to Tapio Korte (personal communication). Also, I thank an anonymous referee of GPS for many useful suggestions that improved this paper.

References

Bealer, George 2002: "Modal Epistemology and the Rationalist Renaissance". In: Tamar S. Gendler & John Hawthorne (eds.), *Conceivability and Possibility*. Oxford: Oxford University Press, 71–125.

Dummett, Michael 1973: *Frege: Philosophy of Language*. London: Duckworth.

Evans, Gareth 1982: *The Varieties of Reference*. Oxford: Oxford University Press.

Frege, Gottlob 1884: *Die Grundlagen der Arithmetik: Eine logisch mathematische Untersuchung über den Begriff der Zahl / The Foundations of Arithmetic: A Logico-Mathematical Enquiry into the Concept of Number*. Trans. John L. Austin. Oxford: Blackwell. Second, revised ed. 1953 (first ed. 1950). = GL

— 1967: *Kleine Schriften*. Ed. Ignacio Angelelli. Hildesheim: G. Olms. = KS

— 1969: *Nachgelassene Schriften*. Ed. Hans Hermes, Friedrich Kambartel & Friedrich Kaulbach. Hamburg: Felix Meiner. Second, revised ed. 1983. = NS

— 1979: *Posthumous Writings*. Ed. Hans Hermes, Friedrich Kambartel & Friedrich Kaulbach, trans. Peter Long & Roger White. Oxford: Blackwell. = PW

— 1984: *Collected Papers on Mathematics, Logic, and Philosophy*. Ed. Brian McGuinness, trans. Hans Kaal *et al*. Oxford: Blackwell. = CP

Kaplan, David 1989: "Demonstratives: An Essay on the Semantics, Logic, Metaphysics, and Epistemology of Demonstratives and Other Indexicals". In: Joseph Almog, John Perry & Howard Wettstein (eds.), *Themes from Kaplan*. Oxford: Oxford University Press, 481–563.

Kripke, Saul 1979: "A Puzzle about Belief". In: Avishai Margalit (ed.), *Meaning and Use*. Dordrecht: Reidel, 239–83.

— 1980: *Naming and Necessity*. Cambridge: Harvard University Press.

DIE MORALPILLE – ÜBER RISIKEN UND NEBENWIRKUNGEN DENKEN SIE EIGENSTÄNDIG NACH UND FRAGEN IHREN PHILOSOPHEN ODER IHRE PHILOSOPHIN

Dorothee BLEISCH
Friedrich-Alexander-Universität Erlangen-Nürnberg

Winner of the first prize of the 2014 essay competition for students sponsored by the *Gesellschaft für Analytische Philosophie* (GAP) in cooperation with the *Grazer Philosophische Studien**

Abstract

This paper discusses whether in principle a pill could exist that turned us into morally better persons and whether we should take such a pill. To answer these questions I will first analyse what being a "morally good person" and further becoming a "morally better person" means. I will particularly spell out three different conditions that a morally good person has to fulfil. I will then argue that a person can be improved in only some of these conditions by taking a pill. Finally, I will show that even if one can become a morally better person by taking the moral pill, it is far from obvious that one should take it. Taking the moral pill would bring with it risks and side effects one should consider thoroughly.

1. *Einleitung*

Stellen Sie sich vor, jemand bietet Ihnen eine Pille an, mit dem Versprechen, dass diese Pille Sie moralischer machen wird. Wie reagieren Sie? – Wahrscheinlich halten Sie die Person für einen unseriösen Quacksalber und lehnen das Angebot irritiert ab. Angenommen aber, dass die Person eine renommierte Forscherin ist. Wie reagieren Sie jetzt und wie *sollten* Sie reagieren? Sicher ist es doch wünschenswert, dass jeder von uns moralischer wird, als er oder sie augenblicklich

---

* The question of the 2014 competition was: "The pill that makes us morally better: can there be such a pill and should we take it?" From the 25 submissions that conformed to the rules of the competition, the jury selected three, one each for the first, second, and third prize. The authors of the prizewinning essays were permitted to slightly revise and expand their submissions for publication.

ist. Wenn sich Ihnen nun eine solche Möglichkeit bietet, sollten Sie dann diese Gelegenheit nicht ergreifen? Aber ist es überhaupt denkbar, dass es eine solche Pille gibt? – Das geschilderte Szenario führt zu den beiden zentralen Fragen dieses Essays: (F1) *Kann* es eine Pille geben, die uns moralischer macht, und (F2) *sollten* wir sie nehmen?

Auf die Fragen F1 und F2 möchte ich im Folgenden eine erste Antwort finden. Bevor ich mit der Diskussion der zentralen Fragen beginne, ist es jedoch wichtig, F1 zu präzisieren, da zwei Lesarten der ersten Frage möglich sind. Dass uns etwas – bspw. eine Pille – moralischer macht, könnte nämlich erstens heißen, dass die Pille dazu führt, dass wir eine größere Anzahl an moralisch richtigen Handlungen ausführen. Zweitens könnte es aber auch heißen, dass die Pille uns zu moralischeren Personen macht. Diese beiden Lesarten sind voneinander verschieden, da sich eine moralisch gute Person – wie ich im zweiten Abschnitt zeigen werde – nicht ausschließlich durch moralisch richtiges Handeln charakterisieren lässt. Ich werde F1 im Sinne der zweiten Lesart verstehen. Es wird im Folgenden also um die Fragen gehen, ob es eine Pille geben kann, die uns *zu moralisch besseren Personen* macht, und ob wir eine solche Pille nehmen sollten.

Um diese Fragen beantworten zu können, muss man sich überlegen, was es heißt, eine *moralische* Person zu sein, und was es bedeutet, dass eine Person morali*scher* ist als eine andere Person bzw. moralischer im Vergleich zu einem früheren, weniger moralischen Zeitpunkt. Diese Begriffsklärungen sind besonders zur Beantwortung von F1 zentral, da sie einen Ansatz liefern, wie sich eine Person verändern müsste, um moralischer zu werden. Erst dann kann man klären, wie eine Moralpille funktionieren müsste und ob es eine solche Pille überhaupt geben könnte. Ich werde hierbei verschiedene Bedingungen herausarbeiten, welche eine moralisch gute Person erfüllen muss (vgl. Abschnitt 2). Im Anschluss daran werde ich diskutieren, inwiefern es eine Pille geben kann, die uns in Hinsicht auf diese Bedingungen verbessert. Ich werde dafür argumentieren, dass es zwar eine Pille geben kann, die uns in beschränkter Hinsicht zu moralisch besseren Personen macht, es aber keine Pille geben kann, die uns in jeglicher Hinsicht, d.h. in Bezug auf alle Bedingungen, zu moralisch besseren Personen macht (vgl. Abschnitt 3). Nimmt man an, dass Sollen Können impliziert, d.h. hier, dass man die Pille nur einnehmen soll, wenn man sie auch einnehmen kann, und geht man weiter davon aus, dass man die Pille nur einnehmen kann, wenn es diese Pille geben kann, so ist durch die Beantwortung der ersten Frage auch F2 zum Teil beantwortet: Eine Pille, die uns moralischer macht, kann es nur geben, wenn wir bereits bestimmte Bedingungen erfüllen, und nur unter diesen Umständen können wir uns sinnvollerweise fragen, ob wir eine solche Pille nehmen sollten. Abschließend möchte ich zeigen, dass es selbst in den Fällen, in denen die

Einnahme der Pille uns moralischer machen würde, sehr fragwürdig ist, ob wir eine solche Pille nehmen sollten (vgl. Abschnitt 4).

2. Begriffsklärungen – Was heißt es, eine moralische Person zu sein?

In der Alltagssprache spricht man oft von einer Vielzahl von „Moralen" und versteht unter *einer Moral* „ein komplexes Ganzes aus teils kollektiv geteilten, teils individuellen und gruppenspezifisch ausdifferenzierten Überzeugungen über richtiges Handeln und entsprechende Forderungen" (Birnbacher 2013, 7). Eine bestimmte Moral ist demnach ein ganz bestimmter Komplex aus Überzeugungen und Forderungen, welche Handlungen auszuführen und welche zu unterlassen sind. Ein wichtiges Kennzeichen von Moral ist – wie in der Definition deutlich wird – der Handlungsbezug, d.h. im Mittelpunkt von Moral stehen Urteile, durch die Handlungen positiv oder negativ bewertet werden.

Auch für die Frage, was eine Person zu einer „moralischen" Person macht, ist dieser Handlungsbezug entscheidend. So werden „Personen [...] als moralisch löblich oder verwerflich beurteilt, in dem Maße, in dem sie in der Regel zu moralisch zu billigendem oder missbilligendem Handeln führen" (Birnbacher 2013, 12-13). Eine Person wäre folglich in dem Maße moralisch, in dem sie in der Regel die moralisch richtigen Handlungen ausführt. Eine Person ist demnach moralisch*er* als eine andere oder in Bezug auf einen früheren Zeitpunkt, wenn sie mehr richtige Handlungen ausführt bzw. weniger falsche Handlungen.[1]

Moralisch richtiges Handeln ist aber noch kein hinreichendes Kriterium, um eine Person als moralisch gut oder schlecht zu beurteilen. Denn eine Person kann aus den falschen Gründen motiviert sein, moralisch richtige Handlungen auszuführen. So handelt jemand, der einem anderen nur aufgrund negativer (Strafe) oder positiver Maßnahmen (Belohnung) hilft, durchaus moralisch richtig, ist aber deswegen noch keine moralisch gute Person (vgl. Mill 1861, 150–152), da er nicht angemessen motiviert ist.

Es gibt verschiedene Auffassungen davon, was es heißt, angemessen motiviert zu sein (vgl. zu den unterschiedlichen Auffassungen Olson 2002). Gewöhnlich gehen die Auffassungen von zwei verschiedenen Motivationstypen, der sog. *de dicto* und der sog. *de re Motivation*, aus. *De dicto* motiviert ist eine Person, wenn sie motiviert ist, das (moralisch) Richtige auszuführen, was auch immer es ist. Dieser Fall läge z.B. vor, wenn eine Person motiviert ist, einen Ertrinkenden zu retten, weil sie das Richtige tun möchte und davon überzeugt ist, dass die Handlung die Eigenschaft besitzt, moralisch richtig zu sein. *De re* motiviert ist eine

---

1. Wichtig ist hierbei, dass das moralisch Richtige nicht mit dem zusammenfallen muss, was in einem bestimmten Moralsystem geboten ist.

Person hingegen, wenn sie aus der Sache selbst heraus motiviert ist, d.h. wenn sie durch ihre Sorge um das Objekt der Handlung (ertrinkende Person) motiviert ist. Wenn die handelnde Person *de re motiviert* ist, bspw. den Ertrinkenden zu retten, dann rettet sie ihn, weil sie sich direkt um den Ertrinkenden sorgt. Die Überlegung, dass die Handlung die Eigenschaft besitzt, eine moralisch richtige zu sein, spielt in der *de re Motivation* keine Rolle (vgl. zur Unterscheidung von *de dicto* und *de re* Carbonell 2013).

Ein erster Ansatz geht nun davon aus, dass eine Person dann und nur dann angemessen motiviert ist, wenn sie *ausschließlich de dicto motiviert* ist, das Richtige zu tun. Moralische Personen sind demnach motiviert, Handlungen allein um ihrer (moralischen) Richtigkeit willen auszuführen. Kritiker dieses Ansatzes bezeichnen solche Personen jedoch als „moralische Fetischisten" (vgl. Smith 1994, Kapitel 4) und bemängeln, dass solche Personen nicht durch Sorge um die Notleidenden selbst motiviert sind. Sie vertreten deswegen die entgegengesetzte Position, wonach Personen dann und nur dann angemessen motiviert sind, wenn sie *ausschließlich de re motiviert* sind, das Richtige zu tun. Nach diesem Ansatz sind die angemessen motivierten Personen nicht motiviert, die moralisch richtigen Handlungen auszuführen, weil die Handlungen unter die Kategorie „moralisch richtig" fallen, sondern weil die Personen sich z.B. um das Wohlergehen der notleidenden Person sorgen und überzeugt sind, dass die Handlungen das Wohlergehen der leidenden Personen verbessern.

Beide Ansätze sind meines Erachtens nicht überzeugend. Der erste Ansatz ist nicht überzeugend, da es nicht ersichtlich ist, warum eine Person unangemessen motiviert sein sollte, wenn sie nicht nur danach strebt, das Richtige zu tun, sondern auch durch Sorge um die Notleidenden selbst motiviert wird. Umgekehrt gilt aber auch, dass es nicht ersichtlich ist, warum eine Person unangemessen motiviert sein sollte, wenn sie nicht nur – z.B. aufgrund ihres Mitleides mit der leidenden Person – *de re*, sondern auch *de dicto motiviert* ist, das Richtige zu tun.[2] Denn dass eine Person sich beim Handeln nicht allein auf ihre jeweilige *de re Motivation* verlässt, sondern auch *de dicto motiviert* ist, das Richtige zu tun und gegebenenfalls Überlegungen anstellt, ob die von ihr gewünschten Handlungen tatsächlich moralisch richtig sind, ist ein Zeichen von Reflektiertheit. Es ist nicht klar, warum Reflektiertheit der Moralität einer Person abträglich sein sollte. Im Gegenteil ist eine Person meines Erachtens angemessen motiviert, wenn sie *sowohl* aufgrund ihrer Sorge um die betreffenden Personen *als auch* aufgrund ihrer Sorge um das moralisch Richtige motiviert ist, da nur dann sichergestellt ist, dass sie bei ihren Handlungen sowohl unparteiischen Überlegungen als auch das Wohl einzelner Personen angemessen berücksichtigt.

---

2. Das heißt nicht unbedingt, dass eine solche Person bei jeder Handlung zunächst überlegen muss, ob die Handlung auch moralisch richtig ist (vgl. hierzu bspw. Railton 1984).

Es stellt sich die Frage, ob nicht allein die angemessene Motivation hinreichend ist, um eine Person als moralisch gut zu kennzeichnen. Kann nicht auch eine Person, die immer optimal motiviert ist, deren Handlungen aber katastrophale Auswirkungen haben, als moralisch gut bezeichnet werden? Es ist an dieser Stelle wichtig, zwischen vorhersehbaren und nicht vorhersehbaren Handlungsfolgen zu unterscheiden. Vorhersehbare Handlungsfolgen sind der Person anzulasten, unvorhersehbare hingegen nicht. Dies lässt sich an Beispielen verdeutlichen. So könnte man sich z.B. vorstellen, dass Person A ihren Gästen, ohne dies zu bemerken, verdorbenes Essen zubereitet, woraufhin diese krank werden. Nimmt man an, dass Person A die schlechten Folgen ihrer Handlung leicht hätte erkennen können, wenn sie aufmerksamer gewesen wäre, so gibt die Tatsache, dass die Person die Handlung ausgeführt hat, Aufschluss über den moralischen Charakter der Person (vgl. zu einem ähnlichen Beispiel Sinnott-Armstrong 2014, Gliederungspunkt 4). Anders sieht es aus, wenn die Folgen der Handlung für die Person nicht vorhersehbar waren. So könnte man sich z.B. vorstellen, dass einer der Gäste an einer äußerst seltenen Allergie leidet von der bisher niemand etwas wusste. Dieser Gast erleidet aufgrund des Essens einen allergischen Schock. In diesem Fall scheint es absurd, Person A als moralisch schlecht zu bezeichnen. Unvorhersehbare Folgen sind einer Person also nicht anzulasten. Wären alle Folgen der Handlungen unvorhersehbar, dann könnte man demnach in der Tat die Person trotz missglückter Handlungen als moralisch gut bezeichnen. Es ist aber unwahrscheinlich, dass dies für alle Handlungen der Person zutrifft. Wie gut eine Person moralisch ist, hängt demnach auch von der Qualität der Handlungen der Person ab. Erst der Komplex aus Handlungen und Motivation zusammengenommen bildet die Beurteilungsgrundlage für die Moralität der Person.

Sind diese beiden Bedingungen zusammengenommen nun hinreichend, um eine moralische Person zu charakterisieren? – Nein. So kann man sich eine Person A vorstellen, die aufgrund glücklicher Umstände stets richtig handelt und intuitiv angemessen motiviert ist, ohne zu verstehen, warum die ausgeführte Handlung richtig ist und ohne eigenständig Zusammenhänge zwischen moralisch relevanten Aspekten durchdenken und erkennen zu können. Einer solchen Person fehlt moralisches Verständnis. Vergleicht man diesen moralischen Glückspilz (Person A) nun mit einer Person B, die auch moralisches Verständnis besitzt, d.h. nicht nur richtig handelt und angemessen motiviert ist, sondern auch verstehen kann, warum die ausgeführte Handlung richtig ist und *eigenständig* Zusammenhänge zwischen moralisch relevanten Aspekten durchdenken und erkennen kann, so scheint Person B moralisch besser als Person A. Eine moralisch gute Person sollte idealiter also auch *moralisches Verständnis* besitzen.

Zusammenfassend lässt sich sagen, dass eine Person moralisch gut ist, wenn sie (i) in der Regel moralisch richtig handelt, (ii) angemessen motiviert ist und

(iii) moralisches Verständnis besitzt. Es gilt dabei, dass eine Person in dem Maße moralisch besser, d.h. moralischer ist, je umfassender sie die drei Bedingungen – richtiges Handeln, angemessene Motivation und moralisches Verständnis – erfüllt. Eine Pille, die uns *vollumfänglich* zu moralisch besseren Personen macht, müsste demnach dazu führen, dass wir in Hinsicht auf *alle* drei Bedingungen besser werden. Erfüllen wir bereits einen Teil der Bedingungen, so könnte uns aber auch eine Pille moralischer machen, die nur bewirkt, dass wir in Hinblick auf die restliche(n) Bedingung(en) besser werden.

3. Diskussion – Kann es die Moralpille geben?

Ich werde im Folgenden diskutieren, inwiefern die drei Bedingungen, welche eine moralische Person erfüllen muss, medikamentös verbessert werden könnten.

Kann es eine Pille geben, die bewirkt, dass wir mehr richtige Handlungen ausführen? Für die Diskussion der ersten Bedingung ist es hilfreich sich zu fragen, warum und auf welche Weise Menschen falsch handeln. Man kann auf zwei verschiedene Weisen falsch handeln: *entweder* man handelt falsch, weil man aus Willensschwäche nicht tut, was man als richtig erkannt hat, *oder* man handelt falsch, weil man nicht weiß, was richtig ist bzw. sich darin irrt, was richtig ist (vgl. Ernst 2012, 39). Eine Pille, die bewirkt, dass wir mehr richtige Handlungen ausführen, müsste also unsere Willensschwäche minimieren oder uns moralisches Wissen einflößen.

Kann es eine Pille geben, die unsere Willensschwäche minimiert? Dies möchte ich an einem extrem Fallbeispiel diskutieren. In der *Zeit* vom 25.10.2012 wurde von einem Mann berichtet, der pädophile Neigungen besitzt (aber noch nie übergriffig geworden war) und seine Neigungen sowie sexuellen Kontakt mit Kindern selbst als moralisch falsch beurteilt. Dem Mann wurde von Ärzten ein Medikament verschrieben, das seinen Hormonlevel senkte und so jegliche sexuelle Neigungen unterdrückte. In diesem Fall kann man durchaus sagen, dass das Medikament diesem Mann erleichterte, nicht aus Willensschwäche furchtbare Handlungen auszuführen (vgl. Faller 2012, 1-12). Es sind also Medikamente denkbar, die uns, sofern wir angemessen motiviert sind, moralisches Verständnis besitzen und wissen, was richtig ist, zu moralischeren Personen machen, indem sie unsere Willensschwäche reduzieren.

Sind auch Medikamente vorstellbar, die unser moralisches Wissen erweitern?[3] Man könnte dies zurückweisen, indem man argumentiert, dass der Erwerb von

---

3. Unter „moralischem Wissen" verstehe ich hier nicht nur im engen Sinne wahre Überzeugungen über den deontischen Status der bewerteten Sache, z.B. eine wahre Überzeugung darüber, dass Handlung X richtig ist, sondern im weiten Sinne jede Form des Wissens, das für die Bestimmung des moralischen Status der Handlung relevant ist.

Wissen immer eine aktive Benutzung des eigenen Verstandes erfordert. Diese Annahme scheint allerdings zu stark, da nicht jede Form des Wissenszuwachses eine aktive Benutzung des eigenen Verstandes voraussetzt. Legt bspw. jemand meine Hand auf einen warmen Heizkörper, so spüre ich die Wärme des Heizkörpers und gelange folglich zu dem Wissen, dass der Heizkörper warm ist, ohne eine anspruchsvolle, aktive Überlegung angestellt zu haben.

Man könnte zweitens auch bestreiten, dass Wissen medikamentös eingeflößt werden kann, indem man argumentiert, dass der Erwerb von Wissen zwangsläufig auf „echten Erfahrungen", d.h. auf Sinneswahrnehmungen von Dingen, die außerhalb unseres Geistes existieren oder stattfinden, basieren muss. Dieses Argument kann man jedoch entkräften, indem man argumentiert, dass nicht jedes Wissen auf „echten Erfahrungen" basieren muss. So erweitert auch die Erfahrung, dass Person A auf ein bestimmtes Medikament allergisch reagiert oder die Einnahme einer Droge bei Person B Angstzustände verursacht, das Wissen der Personen über sich selbst. Meines Erachtens kann man also prinzipiell *nicht* ausschließen, dass die Einnahme von Medikamenten zu einem Wissenszuwachs führt. Allerdings handelt es sich bei moralischem Wissen nicht nur um Wissen über die Person selbst. Moralisches Wissen basiert vielmehr zum größten Teil auf Sinneswahrnehmungen von Dingen, die außerhalb unseres Geistes existieren oder stattfinden. Ein Beispiel hierfür wäre das Wissen darum, dass andere Lebewesen schmerzempfindlich sind. Ein solches Wissen ist moralisch relevant, kann aber nur durch die Beobachtung anderer, d.h. durch „echte Erfahrungen" gewonnen werden.[4] Demnach kann höchstens ein kleiner Teil des moralisch relevanten Wissens eingeflößt werden. Es ist folglich unwahrscheinlich, dass uns Wissen in solchem Umfang eingeflößt werden kann, dass wir wahre Meinungen über den deontischen Status unserer Handlungen gewinnen.

Ich komme nun zur zweiten Bedingung und erörtere, inwiefern es eine Pille geben kann, die bewirkt, dass wir angemessener motiviert sind. Wie ich im zweiten Abschnitt argumentiert habe, ist eine Person angemessenen motiviert, wenn sie sowohl *de re* als auch *de dicto* motiviert ist. So müsste bspw. bei einer Person A, die ausschließlich motiviert ist, einen Ertrinkenden zu retten, weil sie dadurch Ansehen erlangt, diese Motivation verändert werden, damit man sagen kann, dass Person A angemessen motiviert ist. Kann eine solche Änderung der

---

4. An dieser Stelle könnte man einwenden, dass Medikamente zwar keine „echten Erfahrungen" liefern, sie uns aber empfänglicher für bestimmte Sachverhalte machen können. Sind wir empfänglicher für bestimmte Sachverhalte, so gelangen wir auch zu Wissen, dass wir ohne Einnahme der Pille nicht besessen hätten. Allerdings scheitert diese Strategie, da uns solche Medikamente nicht direkt moralisches Wissen einflößen, sondern nur erleichtern, dieses Wissen zu erlangen.

Motivationsstruktur medikamentös herbeigeführt werden? Es ist an dieser Stelle wichtig, sich zu überlegen, was es heißt, dass eine Person auf eine bestimmte Weise motiviert ist, und was notwendig ist, um diese Motivationsstruktur zu ändern. Eine Person ist nur dann motiviert, d.h. willig eine Handlung auszuführen, wenn sie die normative Überzeugung besitzt, dass die Handlung oder ein Aspekt der Handlung gut ist. Eine Person kann dabei durchaus aufgrund verschiedener Überzeugungen eine komplexe Motivationsstruktur mit unterschiedlichen Motivationen aufweisen. Eine Änderung in der Motivationsstruktur tritt demnach nur dann ein, wenn eine Überzeugung aufgegeben wird oder neu hinzukommt. Inwiefern es eine Pille geben kann, die unsere Motivation verbessert, hängt also davon ab, ob Überzeugungen passiv – bspw. durch Medikamente – geändert werden können. Diesen Punkt habe ich bereits im Rahmen der Frage, inwiefern moralisches Wissen, d.h. wahre Überzeugungen, medikamentös erweitert werden kann, diskutiert. Dort zeigte sich, dass Wissen prinzipiell medikamentös erweitert und somit auch verändert werden kann. Es ist also grundsätzlich nicht auszuschließen, dass Änderungen der Überzeugungen und folglich der Motivation auch auf biochemischer Ebene durch ein Medikament verursacht werden könnten. Allerdings zeigte sich dort auch, dass bestimmtes (moralisches) Wissen sich einer solchen Einflößung zu widersetzen scheint, da es auf echten Erfahrungen basiert. Demnach ist es auch im Falle der Motivationsänderung unwahrscheinlich, dass diese derart geändert werden können, sodass wir angemessener motiviert sind.

Es bleibt noch die dritte Bedingung zu diskutieren: Kann es eine Pille geben, die unser moralisches Verständnis vertieft? Es ist nun nicht vorstellbar, dass ein solches moralisches Verständnis medikamentös eingeflößt oder vertieft werden kann. Denn ein moralisches Verständnis zu besitzen bedeutet, dass die Person in der Lage ist, eigenständig Zusammenhänge zu durchdenken und Beziehungen zwischen verschiedenen Tatsachen herzustellen. Moralisches Verständnis kann demnach auch nur vertieft werden, indem die Person *eigenständig* Zusammenhänge durchdenkt und sich aktiv ihres Verstandes bedient. Die Vertiefung moralischen Verständnisses ist also eine Aufgabe, die prinzipiell nicht von einer Pille übernommen werden kann.

4. *Fazit – Sollen wir die Moralpille nehmen?*

Wie ich in der Einleitung betont habe, ist F2 nur sinnvoll, sofern wir auch die Möglichkeit haben, eine solche Pille zu nehmen. Nach meiner Analyse stellt sich F2 also in erster Linie, wenn wir angemessen motiviert sind, moralisches Verständnis besitzen, aber unter Willensschwäche leiden. Ich möchte im Folgenden jedoch auch darauf eingehen, ob wir im Fall der Wissenserweiterung und der Motivationsverbesserung eine solche Pille nehmen sollten, da es auch hier zumindest prinzipiell möglich ist, dass es eine Moralpille geben könnte.

Auf den ersten Blick besteht ein scheinbar zwingendes Argument für die Einnahme dieser Moralpille. So ist es schwer zu bestreiten, dass wir moralisch so gut wie möglich sein sollten. Folglich scheint es moralisch geboten, dass wir die Moralpille nehmen, wenn dies möglich ist. Trotz dieser scheinbar zwingenden Argumentation bleibt ein Unbehagen gegenüber der Einnahme der Moralpille bestehen. Dieses Unbehagen rührt vor allem daher, dass eine solche Pille unser Wissen bestimmen und unsere Motivation regulieren würde. Diese Pille müsste unser Denken übernehmen und die Funktion analog zu einer Maschine oder eines Menschen annehmen, der für uns denkt und für uns handelt. Dies würde letztendlich zur Verkümmerung unseres ganzen Selbst und damit auch zum Verlust unserer Autonomie führen. Denn der eigene Verstand und das angemessene moralische Verständnis kann nur durch Betätigung des eigenen Verstandes trainiert werden. Bei der Frage nach der Einnahme der Moralpille gilt es also, verbesserte Moralität gegen geringere Autonomie bzw. Aufgabe der eigenen Autonomie abzuwägen; eine Abwägung, die nicht pauschal vorgenommen werden kann und deren Ausgang nicht von vornherein feststeht. So mag es Fälle wie den pädophiler Neigungen geben, in denen wir wahrscheinlich die medikamentöse Hilfestellung annehmen sollten, da die betroffenen Neigungen zu große Risiken für andere bergen. In anderen Fällen scheint es hingegen nicht gerechtfertigt, für höhere Moralität die eigene Autonomie aufzugeben. Es ist des Weiteren zu beachten, dass Medikamente nur eine Art der Hilfe – und wahrscheinlich nicht einmal die beste Art – darstellen. Jene anderen Formen der Hilfe, wie z.B. die Unterstützung durch Freunde, wären meines Erachtens vorzuziehen, wenn sie dieselbe Wirkung haben, ohne unsere Autonomie einzuschränken. Fragen Sie also, ob Sie die angenommene Pille nehmen sollten, dann kann man Ihnen wohl nur äußerste Skepsis ans Herz legen und raten: „Bedenken Sie die Situation eigenständig!"[5]

---

5. Ebenfalls hilfreich ist es, diese Frage mit anderen zu diskutieren. Für hilfreiche Diskussionen und Kommentare zu diesem Essay bedanke ich mich besonders bei Dr. Christian Seidel. Zudem bedanke ich mich für Anmerkungen bei Florian Dobmeier, Sebastian Schmidt, Prof. Thomas Schramme, Konstantin Weber und den Jurymitgliedern.

Literatur

Birnbacher, Dieter 2013³: *Analytische Einführung in die Ethik*. Berlin, Boston: Walter de Gruyter.

Carbonell, Vanessa 2013: „De Dicto Desires and Morality as Fetish". *Philosophical Studies* 163, 459–477

Ernst, Gerhard 2012: *Denken wie ein Philosoph, Eine Anleitung in sieben Tagen*. München: Pantheon.

Faller, Heike 2012: „Der Getriebene". *Zeit online*, 25.10.2012, abgerufen unter: http://www.zeit.de/2012/44/Sexualitaet-Paedophilie-Therapie (Stand: 15.10.2014).

Mill, John Stuart 1861/2008: „Utilitarianism". In: John Gray (Hg.), *On Liberty and Other Essays*. Oxford/New York: Oxford University Press, 129–201.

Olson, Jonas 2002: „Are Desires De Dicto Fetishistic?". *Inquiry* 45, 89–96.

Railton, Peter 1984: „Alienation, Consequentialism, and the Demands of Morality". *Philosophy & Public Affairs* 13, 134–171.

Sinnott-Armstrong 2014: „Consequentialism". In: Zalta, Edward (Hg.), *The Stanford Encyclopedia of Philosophy*. Abgerufen unter: http://plato.stanford.edu/archives/spr2014/entries/consequentialism/.

Smith, Michael 1994: *The Moral Problem*. Oxford, Cambridge: Blackwell.

AGENCY & THE PILL THAT MAKES US MORAL

Philip FOX
University of Bayreuth

Winner of the second prize of the 2014 essay competition for students sponsored by the *Gesellschaft für Analytische Philosophie* (GAP) in cooperation with the *Grazer Philosophische Studien**

Abstract
Can there be a pill that makes us more moral? This paper argues, first, that *S* increases her degree of morality by taking a magic pill only if the pill's influence is compatible with the idea that *S* satisfies moral requirements. Second, given the complex way in which morality both presupposes and protects agential capacities, it follows that a necessary condition for *S* to satisfy moral requirements is for *S* to be an agent. The paper then considers two possible mechanics of the pill and shows how opposite assessments regarding the possibility of the pill follow, depending on how exactly it affects someone's agential capacities.

1. Introduction

Can there be a pill that makes us more moral and, if yes, ought we to take it? A preliminary first. I assume that the answer to the latter question is trivial once we know the answer to the former. The reason is this: Most people accept that morality is normative. That is, we typically assume that morality defines norms of conduct that we have reason to comply with. Hence, if there is a pill that makes us more moral and we accept the normativity of morality, then we have a reason to take it. If this reason outweighs any reason to the contrary, we ought

---

* The question of the 2014 competition was: "The pill that makes us morally better: can there be such a pill and should we take it?" From the 25 submissions that conformed to the rules of the competition, the jury selected three, one each for the first, second, and third prize. The authors of the prizewinning essays were permitted to slightly revise and expand their submissions for publication.

to take the pill[1]. A plausible explanation for our yet hesitating attitude towards taking the pill, then, is that we hesitate to believe that there could be such a pill. To anticipate, the reason is that while we assume individuals to be subject to moral requirements, we also think that individuals must perform morally required actions *in the right way* to satisfy the corresponding requirements. If it turns out that the pill makes one perform morally required actions *in the wrong way*, we may not want to say that the pill makes one more moral. Consequently, the main aim of this essay is to investigate the qualification *in the right way* and to clarify whether it speaks against the possibility of the pill.

I proceed as follows. I begin with a brief account of what it means to possess the property of morality. Put roughly, to be moral is to satisfy moral requirements. To satisfy moral requirements, in turn, is to perform morally required actions in the right way. I continue by investigating the notion of *in the right way* and, in particular, the idea that a necessary condition for performing required actions in the right way is to possess *agency*. After outlining how morality both presupposes and protects effective agential capacities, I use the notion of agency as the basis for my discussion whether the pill could exist. More precisely, I outline two possible mechanics of the pill and examine whether these are compatible with agency, understood as a necessary condition of morality. In the first case, I argue that the pill does not make one more moral, because it is incompatible with an understanding of ourselves as self-governed, moral agents. In the second case, however, the pill only assists self-governed individuals in achieving their own moral plans and hence can make one more moral. I conclude that the possibility of the pill that makes us moral hinges crucially on how it affects our agency, which explains why thinking about hypothetical pills can contribute to our understanding of the relation between agency and morality.

2. *Can the pill exist?*

First, let me specify what I mean by *morality*. In this essay, I focus on morality in the *property sense* rather than the *source sense*[2]. That is, I take morality to be a property of a subject rather than a source that issues requirements to

---

1. For simplification, I assume that no significant reason to the contrary exists. I am not concerned here with cases where one may have reason not to be moral (e.g. a Hobbesian state of nature).

Furthermore, if you do not believe that morality is normative, then, trivially, the answer to the question whether the pill ought to be taken is 'no'. I bracket skepticism about the normativity of morality here.

2. See Broome (2013, Ch. 7) for this distinction.

act in certain ways. The property sense is fundamental to the question whether there can be a pill that *makes us more moral*, i.e. gives us the property of morality. What does it take someone to possess this property? I propose the following account.

A subject S's degree of morality is increased if and only if S satisfies a moral requirement. To satisfy a moral requirement is to perform a morally required action in the right way. Consequently, S's degree of morality does *not* increase if (i) S performs an action[3] that S is morally required not to perform or (ii) S performs a morally required action in the wrong way[4]. Put differently, (ii) expresses the idea that the mere performance of a morally required action *ipso facto* is insufficient to make one more moral. Is this demand too high? It is not. Too see why, consider the following example in which it is evident that someone can perform morally required actions without increasing one's degree of morality. Suppose Jane deliberates whether or not she shall save a stranger's life simply by cautioning the stranger against an approaching runaway trolley car. To decide this question, Jane flips a fair coin. As it turns out, the coin lands in favour of Jane saving the stranger, and she acts accordingly. Plausibly or by stipulation, Jane is under a moral requirement to save the stranger. Does she satisfy it? We should think that she does not. We should not think that Jane satisfies a moral requirement if the only reason for her saving someone's life is the outcome of a coin toss. She merely performs an action that is incidentally the same as the action *necessary* to satisfy the requirement. However, performing morally required actions by chance is *insufficient* to make her more moral. So, it is innocuous to assume that the pill can exist only if it makes one perform required actions in the right way. Note, however, that this assumption does not commit one to accept overly ambitious standards for the satisfaction of moral requirements. Rather, for my purposes I only need to investigate this necessary condition:

(Agency Condition)
Necessarily, if S satisfies a moral requirement, then S possesses agency.

As satisfying moral requirements is equivalent to increasing one's degree of morality, the possibility of the pill hinges on whether it fulfils this condition.

---

3. Of course, one can also *not* perform *required* actions. To simplify, I take my formulation to cover these cases as well.

4. Plausibly, (i) also causes a *decrease* in morality. To discuss whether the pill can make one *more* moral, however, I do not need this stronger claim.

2.1 *The Relevance of Agency*

Obviously, we do not ascribe morality to stones or grasshoppers, but, at least presently, only to a proper subset of living organisms: human beings. The reason for this is, of course, that stones or grasshoppers are not agents. They are not the kinds of entities that we require to deliberate on the right course of action and to act accordingly. Here, I cannot spell out necessary and sufficient conditions for agency, nor is it clear that such an attempt could be successful. To discuss how the pill influences agency, however, it will suffice to elucidate the notion of agency and its relation to morality as follows. This relation is complex, but even the cursory look that I can offer here reveals how morality both *presupposes* and *protects* effective agential capacities.

First, morality presupposes agential capacities insofar as all the central moral categories, such as reasons, requirements, oughts, obligations, etc., assume an agent who is actively responsive or able to satisfy them. Take, for instance, reasons. Morality offers *practical reasons*, which are *reasons for action*, and hence require a capacity to act in accordance with these reasons. This higher-order capacity comprises many more concrete capacities, such as being able to reflect carefully on various courses of action and their consequences, gather the relevant non-normative information, choose the best means to a chosen end, reason accurately under risk and uncertainty, identify and make a decision in line with the reasons that one takes to be decisive, and, if this capacity is to be effective, be free from systematic and pervasive impediments that make the exercise of one's will impossible. In short, agency is constituted by a basic, sufficiently sophisticated, higher-order capacity to act under the guidance of both theoretical and practical reason. If this capacity is absent or too limited, one is not responsive to moral reasons or principles, and hence not under morality's authority. Importantly, what matters for agency understood as a presupposition of morality is whether a subject *could* exercise this capacity, not whether it *does* so. One cannot free oneself from moral requirements by spontaneously stopping to deliberate and act.

Second, while morality presupposes agency, it also defines a sphere of protection around precisely those agential capacities without which moral requirements would not apply in the first place. This sphere of protection grounds individuals' more concrete moral claims to bodily integrity, minimum provision of goods and education, freedom of thought and expression, etc., without which there could be no effective exercise of agency. This does not mean, however, that agency and morality bootstrap each other into existence. It is not the case that moral principles aim at protecting our agential capacities because it is only when we are agents that we can obey those principles. Morality does not protect these capacities *for the sake* of subjecting us to its principles. That would be a form of moral fetishism. It is rather that there is an independent moral explanation of why our agential capacities are worthy of protection. This explanation is, for instance, that through the exercise of agency we are able to promote happiness in ourselves and others; or that through the exercise of agency we can set to ourselves and achieve ends in accordance with the laws of pure practical reason that are constitutive of our freedom and autonomy, etc., depending on the structure of one's first-order moral theory (teleological, deontological, etc.).

In light of these remarks on the relevance of agency for morality, let me add, however, that my project here cannot be foundationalist. That is, whether or not the reader already accepts the account of the relation between agency and morality given here, one can appraise the moral importance of agency only in conjunction with a detailed case study of how our ascriptions of morality do (not) co-vary with our ascriptions of agency in particular examples, which in turn must feed into any theoretical assessment of the role of agency. Let me turn to such a case study approach in the remainder of this essay.

2.2 *Two Possible Mechanics*

More precisely, let me now outline two possible mechanics of the pill. The first mechanics licenses a clear verdict against the possibility of the pill, as it deprives the individual of her ability to control her life as a self-governed agent. In contrast, the second mechanics is compatible with agency, as it only assists the pill-taker in achieving the moral plans that she wants to achieve anyway. A discussion of these two cases will bring out the central relevance of agency for morality even further.

One way the pill could try to ensure one's morality is this. Suppose S is about to act immorally. Plausibly, the kinds of action that interest us here—beating a child, lying to a friend, donating to charity, helping your neighbour—are always based on corresponding intentions. To simplify, we can therefore assume as a general truth that whenever S ϕ-s, S had a prior intention to ϕ. S's immoral actions are then based on immoral intentions. Whenever S forms such an intention, the pill then interferes with S's mind and replaces the immoral intention with a moral one. To avoid irrationality, it may also add the moral beliefs that cohere with these intentions. As people typically do what they intend to do, an interference operating on intentions generally ensures that S abstains from morally prohibited actions. If, however, S already has a moral intention, the pill does not interfere at all. Given that these processes of mental (non-) interference are unexceptionally reliable, anyone under the influence of the pill ceases to commit prohibited actions. Is this compatible with the satisfaction of moral requirements?

I think it is not. Recall that my interest here is in what makes it the case that someone possesses the property of morality. As I have said, a plausible necessary condition for possessing this property is to be an agent, which requires a basic capacity to act under the guidance of both theoretical and practical reason. In an individual under the influence of this pill, however, the most distinctive constituent of agency, practical reason, is severely compromised. Practical reasoning is, roughly, reasoning that concludes in an intention, or plan of action, which follows coherently from beliefs about one's practical reasons in a given moral environment (cf. Fink 2013, Section 1). This capacity must neither be perfect nor always fully exercised for someone to be an agent, but it is clear that some sufficient degree of control over one's own mental attitudes (beliefs, intentions, desires, etc.) is necessary for someone to be an agent. Otherwise, the main tools that make one favour one action over another and act accordingly are entirely lost.

On any plausible reading of 'sufficient', however, this pill amounts to a serious impediment to the self-governing exercise of practical reason. If, in every situation in which one intends a prohibited action, one's own mental states are radically manipulated by the pill, one gives up a significant part of the control over one's own life. To illustrate, imagine someone with a considerable degree of immorality. This person, committing a non-trivial number of immoral actions, would - via taking the pill - possess a non-trivial number of intentions that are not her own. Of course, she may consider these intentions as genuinely belonging to her, but we know that these are induced by the pill. It seems odd to think of this person as a generally self-governed agent who is morally responsible for her actions.

Even worse, this kind of interference conflicts with the principle *ought implies cannot* (cf. Mill 1985, 379; Fink 2007, 148). Put roughly, this principle says that if it is not the case that S can fail to ϕ, then it is not the case that S ought to ϕ. For example, there cannot be an *ought* such that one ought to obey the laws of nature. Necessarily, given the physical state of our world, one obeys the laws of nature, so it is futile to formulate an ought with this triviality as its content. An ought is a normative notion, normativity aims at guidance, and there is no point in guiding people towards what they will do anyway.

What does this principle imply for the version of the pill at issue? In line with my previous assumption, I disregard cases in which one has a reason not to be moral. What is morally required, then, is what one ought to do. If the pill is reliable enough to prevent one from performing every prohibited action that one could possibly intend, then one cannot fail to do what is morally required.

No matter what immoral intentions one conceives, the pill always replaces them by their moral counterparts. But if that is true, then in those worlds where one takes the pill, it is not the case that one *cannot* perform morally required actions. Correspondingly, in these worlds, it is never the case that one ought to. However, if the pill makes it the case that in those worlds where the pill is taken, no one ever ought to do anything, the ordinary normative concept of morality does not apply anymore. Therefore, persons under the influence of this pill cannot be said to satisfy moral requirements or possess the property of morality. As we have seen, satisfaction requires agency, and the mere performance of morally required actions does not suffice to increase one's degree of morality. Under this mechanics of the pill, we therefore have an answer to our question: The pill does not make one more moral, because it violates the principle *ought implies cannot*, and because it is incompatible with agency as a necessary condition of possessing the property of morality.

Let me now turn to a different possible mechanics of the pill. Under this version, the pill genuinely increases one's degree of morality and hence ought to be taken. To illustrate, consider an agent who has a particularly good understanding of what is morally right and wrong, but is deeply akratic about morally required actions. That is, even though she knows very well what she ought to do, she often fails to intend what she believes she ought to do. As a result, she often fails to act morally, because she lacks the moral intentions to perform these actions in the first place. To remedy this unwelcome trait of hers, she needs to put all her efforts into forming the intentions that follow from her moral beliefs. Yet, due to some features of her overall psychology, she does not always succeed in doing so. By stipulation, however, if she fails to form the intentions that follow from her beliefs, it is not due to lack of effort, but to some psychological trait of hers that she cannot change. Suppose further that she could take a pill that cures her *akrasia* and makes her herself form the intentions that rationally correspond to her moral beliefs.

In this case, the pill implies that she will perform more morally required actions without undesirable violations of her agency[5]. First, her moral beliefs are still the product of her own deliberation. Furthermore, she would act according to these beliefs, if only she did not have the akratic disposition that prevents her from this. One can also assume that she has a strong desire not to be so akratic and to conform more thoroughly to her moral beliefs, but the quirks of her character simply make this impossible. Under these assumptions, the pill

---

5. Because this agent has a particularly good understanding of what is morally right and wrong, the assumption is that curing her *akrasia* also makes her perform more morally required actions *relative to morally prohibited actions* and so increases her degree of morality all things considered.

merely assists her in achieving the moral standards that she wants to, but cannot achieve. It does not, however, stop her from exercising her moral faculty to determine what is morally right. As it is this faculty that eventually determines what actions she performs, she does not give up control over her life as a moral agent.

So this mechanics differs markedly from the previous one that implants just any intentions in one's mind, irrespective of the moral beliefs that one previously held. In particular, the second version of the pill only remedies *akrasia*, i.e. a problem within the mental framework in which an agent's moral convictions evolve and lead to the corresponding actions. If the connection between moral convictions and actions breaks down, it is not incompatible with one's agency if the pill only supports someone in doing what she, after careful reflection, believes that she ought to do. But if the pill ensures this without corrupting one's agency, someone under the influence of this pill does not automatically fail to satisfy moral requirements. In contrast, insofar as this pill assists an agent in performing more morally required actions, this does imply a genuine increase in the agent's morality. Furthermore, this mechanics does not violate *ought implies cannot*. For in this case, it is very well possible for the agent not to perform morally required actions—it only needs to hold that she has immoral beliefs that, in combination with the corresponding immoral intentions as induced by the pill, conclude in immoral actions. Hence, this version of the pill only assists the agent in achieving the moral plans that are, at the fundamental level, already *her* plans. It does not interfere with, but enhances, someone's capacity to be a self-governed agent and can therefore genuinely make someone more moral.

3. *Conclusion*

In this essay, I approached the question whether there can be a pill that makes us more moral. Under my account, to possess the property of morality, one has to satisfy moral requirements. Importantly, the satisfaction of these requirements is twofold. First, one has to perform morally required actions. Second, one has to do so in the right way. To investigate possible interpretations of *in the right way*, I focused on the following necessary condition: Necessarily, if S satisfies a moral requirement, then S possesses agency. This condition originates in how morality both presupposes and protects effective agential capacities. To clarify this condition, I outlined two possible mechanics of the pill and argued for differential assessments of the pill's possibility, depending on the degree to which it interferes with one's agency. If it imposes intentions that are not genuinely one's own, one does not act as a self-governed agent anymore. The pill then also violates the principle *ought implies cannot*. If it only assists in achieving one's moral plans, however, the pill is compatible with one's agency and hence can make one more moral. Surely, there will be many possible mechanics in between that require a thorough discussion of how exactly they influence agency. I hope to have shown, however, that the proposed investigation of the relation between agency and the mechanics of the pill serves as a useful argumentative frame in which these discussions can usefully take place. And of course, from discussing the possibility of the pill we can learn more about the relation between our nature as agents and the moral requirements that both presuppose and protect this agency. Importantly, this holds whether or not there are science-fiction pills in the real world. Insofar as the pill serves as a proxy for all the different means that affect our agency here and now, discussing the possibility of the pill can therefore contribute to a better understanding of the interconnections between agency and morality as they obtain in our non-science-fiction world.[6]

References

Broome, John 2013: *Rationality Through Reasoning*. Hoboken, NJ: Wiley-Blackwell.

Fink, Julian 2007: "Is the Right Prior to the Good?". *South African Journal of Philosophy* 26(2), 143–149.

Fink, Julian 2013: "What Is (Correct) Practical Reasoning?". *Acta Analytica* 28, 471–482.

Mill, John Stuart 1985: "On Nature". In: John M. Robson (ed.), *The Collected Works of John Stuart Mill, Volume X—Essays on Ethics, Religion, and Society*. Introduction by F.E.L Priestley. Toronto: University of Toronto Press; London: Routledge and Kegan Paul, 373–402.

---

6. I thank Jan Grohn for particularly valuable discussions on the topic of this essay.

BREAKING GOOD: IS THERE A PATENT RECIPE FOR COOKING UP THE MORAL PILL?

David HEERING
Humboldt-Universität zu Berlin

Winner of the third prize of the 2014 essay competition for students sponsored by the *Gesellschaft für Analytische Philosophie* (GAP) in cooperation with the *Grazer Philosophische Studien**

Abstract

I ask whether there is a method for influence that has effect across the board such that any agent will responsibly perform more morally right actions for the right reasons after being submitted to it. Such a procedure could be called "the" moral pill. I distinguish a direct and an indirect version of the moral pill, but conclude that both are not possible because they either leave large classes of agents unaffected or interfere with the agent's moral responsibility.

1. *Introduction*

People can become better moral agents throughout their lives by a variety of influences, such as experience or education. This much seems intuitively clear. It appears right to think then that for a large class of agents there is something which can make them more moral[1].

It is a more substantive question whether there is some procedure, such that it is true for a large class of agents that *this* procedure will make them more moral. The latter question inquires into a common element that could underlie all the diverse ways agents can become morally better or, in other words, it inquires

---

1. It is not true for all possible moral agents due to the logical possibility of morally perfect agents, who cannot become more moral as a matter of definition.

* The question of the 2014 competition was: "The pill that makes us morally better: can there be such a pill and should we take it?" From the 25 submissions that conformed to the rules of the competition, the jury selected three, one each for the first, second, and third prize. The authors of the prizewinning essays were permitted to slightly revise and expand their submissions for publication.

into a "patent medicine" that makes agents more moral. I want to ask the more substantive of these questions in this essay. The philosophical hope behind this question is to find out something interesting about morality by identifying an element common to all moral betterment. And we can represent answers to it as giving us a recipe for cooking up a pill that will make *any* person morally better, irrespective of who they are. Hence, the more extra-clauses for certain groups of agents or individuals we will have to include, the less illuminating an answer will be. The project under consideration therefore depends on the possibility of writing a sufficiently unified recipe.

There are several ways to understand "make more moral" here. It could simply mean an increase in virtuousness or moral sensitivity of the agent, but I will assume a stricter interpretation according to which an increase in morality will mean an increase in (responsible) morally right action for the right reasons.

For reference purposes:

(MP) Something is a moral pill only if it increases how often agents who took it (i) responsibly[2] (ii) perform morally right actions (iii) for moral reasons.

The question I want to answer in this essay then is whether there is a pill such that it is true for a large class of agents that taking this pill will make them more moral, or, in other words, whether there is a patent-medicine version of the moral pill. I will try to answer this question in the negative by first distinguishing two versions of what a moral pill could be and then arguing that both fail to provide a sufficiently general way to increase the morality of agents by the standards of (MP), because they leave big classes of agents unaffected.

(MP) above excludes some intuitively implausible versions of a pill, for example a pill that will directly bring about moral actions by purely causal means. It also at least strongly suggests how I will understand the general conception of how moral pills will increase an agent's morality. They will do this, I suppose, by somehow improving the agent's relation to her decisive (as opposed to pro tanto) moral reasons, where I take reasons to be considerations that speak in favor of an action or attitude. This will have to involve *both* an increase in receptivity towards moral reasons (the agent forms new beliefs about her decisive reasons to φ) and an increase in reactivity (the agent acts for those reasons more often).

---

2. This is expected to accommodate different theories of moral responsibility.

2. (A) the ability pill

The ability version of the moral pill is based on the assumption that the best way to comply with (MP) is to have the pill target the agent's *ability to respond to reasons*. I understand this as the dual ability to both be (passively) receptive to reasons and react to them properly. In the following, I will focus on the latter ability. I will understand it as a modal notion in the following way:

> S has the ability to react to reasons to φ iff S φ-s for those reasons in a suitably large set of possible worlds where she intends to φ.

This ability is active, which means the agent is in control of its manifestation by means of intending to exercise it (not necessarily under this description).

I can see three versions of the ability pill so understood: A positive, a negative and a hybrid version combining positive and negative.

The positive version of the pill will increase the ability to react to reasons when ingested.

My modal understanding of the ability allows us to make sense of this increase: An increase in ability is an increase of the possible situations in which the ability is successfully manifested. An archer will get better at archery by training or taking an "archery pill" if the set of possible situations in which she hits the target includes more situations than before the training. Training or pills will have effects on the intrinsic properties of agents that abilities are presumably grounded in, for example certain neural structures of theirs. Pills will increase the set of worlds where the ability is successfully manifested by targeting those areas.

Have we identified an element that could unify all sorts of moral betterment in the positive pill? It seems to me that we have not. For the positive version of the ability pill will leave a central class of agents unaffected: agents who choose not to manifest their ability to react to reasons because they don't want to act morally. These agents are able to react to reasons, they just cannot be bothered by pesky moral action because it interferes with their personal plans. If they take the pill, it *will* increase the set of *possible* circumstances where they manifest the ability, but this will not lead to their moral betterment as defined in (MP) because it will not lead to them performing more right actions in the actual world. That the positive version of the ability pill fails to make these agents morally better seems especially devastating to the project of finding *the* moral pill to me. Agents who don't want to act morally are not some ludicrous fringe case. On the contrary, agents like them are in the forefront of our mind when we ponder a general cure for amorality. Writing the recipe for a pill that will only make agents morally better who already possess all the needed qualities anyway will be like writing a recipe for a pill that makes people more healthy that only works on people who weren't ill in the first place.

The desire not to act morally could be construed as a condition that obstructs the ability to react to reasons. This is because, as I said, the positive pill will change the intrinsic properties of almost every agent thus making the modal claims that make up the ability true. The problem with the desire not to act morally is that it makes it the case that the strengthened ability is never actually exercised. The actual world thus never counts as a world where the agent intends to manifest her ability.

The negative version of the ability pill builds on this thought. What the negative version does is erase all factors that might block, obstruct or mask the manifestation of the ability to react to reasons. Since the desire in question is such a factor, the negative pill will have the intended effect of eliminating the desire in people who choose not to act morally because they don't want to act in this way, thus increasing the number cases in which they act for moral reasons.

But if this is all the moral pill does, then the pill will leave all agents unaffected who do not suffer from such blockages, but could simply be better moral agents because their abilities are underdeveloped. And this will again be a severe impediment for the search for an element that can make most agents morally better.

It is hence natural to opt for a hybrid version of the pill, which has both the effects of the positive and the effects of the negative pill. Since both ranges of effects target properties that are essential to the ability to react to reasons, the hybrid version of the pill will identify a unifying element in what makes persons morally better. And it will have effects that satisfy (MP) for all problem cases we have considered so far.

So the hybrid version of the ability pill is a promising candidate.

Let me nevertheless express my doubts about the hybrid pill's compatibility with (MP). My doubts are based on a worry about how to identify the right kind of blocking conditions while writing the philosophical recipe for the negative part of the hybrid pill. The recipe will have to contain a phrase specifying which obstructing factors the pill will target. Those factors will have to be systematic. There may be agents who happen to choose not to manifest their ability in every single case with no underlying systematic condition that explains this. The pill would have to erase the intention not to manifest the ability in these cases, which would clash with (MP) because it would make it true in the situation that the agent *could not have refrained from acting for reasons.* Agents who cannot but react to moral reasons do not plausibly (i) act responsibly or even (iii) *for* reasons.

I don't regard it as a severe defect that the ability pill cannot, for the reason just rehearsed, affect agents who happen not to act for reasons non-systematically in every instance, because such cases to me seem rare to the point of being contrived.

So the pill will have to target features of an agent's psyche that systematically obstruct her using her ability by bringing about the decision not to manifest, which would otherwise not be present. I surmise that we think that this is unproblematic because we typically identify such systematic elements as pathological features of an agent's psyche. Akratic, compulsive and depressive agents all share systematic features that block the proper manifestation of their abilities, even if the intrinsic features that ground those abilities have been strengthened by ingestion of pills. The phrase in the recipe for such agents may read: *the negative-pill effects will lift all those conditions the agent would want removed if she were fully rational.*

But I worry that some of the cases I had in mind above are such that even if the agent were fully rational, she would not want her desire not to act morally removed. The desire not to act morally may not be pathological in nature. It may not be something the agent regards as foreign to herself and it may itself be grounded in perfectly rational motives. Agents who have chosen to lead a life that affords them maximal pleasure (in the form of some good like money) may regard the manifestation of their ability to react to moral reasons as a substantial hindrance to their goal. Such agents can justifiably believe that their ability to react to moral reasons will not further their ends. Consequently, their rationally ideal selves will presumably still possess the relevant desire.

We could now drop the "rationally ideal self" clause and simply have the pill target all systematic blockages. But as we just saw, many of them may be entirely rational to uphold. The effect of the pill will then count as an illegitimate incursion into the mental layout of an agent, changing her in a way she and her ideally rational self would not want to be changed. I take it that this feature is sufficient to make the pill's effect count as a sort of manipulation of the agent. There is a very strong intuition however, that this sort of manipulation robs agents of their moral responsibility (see Pereboom 2001 for an argument to this effect that operates with an even weaker notion of manipulation). So again, the hybrid pill will not count as a moral pill as specified by (MP) for agents who have the rational desire not to act morally. Specifically, the fact that the negative effect of the pill will target their desire and thus manipulate them will clash with (i), the responsibility condition in (MP).

One might not share my worry for two reasons: First, maybe people who hold such desires are fringe-cases in the same way that people who never happen to act for moral reasons are. I can only report that I don't share this feeling. Second, a more substantial account of rationality might render the result that the desire not to act morally is not rational after all. But this victory would come at a high cost, for the viability of the pill-account would then depend on the truth of this account of rationality.

The preliminary conclusion for this section is then that the ability pill is either compatible with (MP) but not with the endeavor to find a unified account of the moral pill or compatible with this endeavor but too "strong" to be compatible with (MP).

These failures might incline us to look for another way to cook up a moral pill that complies with (MP) and the notion of a unified formula for the pill.

3. (B) the direct pill

The direct version might offer such an account. Direct pills do not take a detour via abilities to increase the agent's morality. Instead, they directly influence agents in accordance with (MP) by adding new true beliefs about what the agent ought to do. My argument against this sort of pill will consists in showing that this pill-conception is inconsistent with a plausible assumption about the truth-conditions of ought-beliefs:

(1) For any morally non-perfect agent A, the direct pill will causally influence the agent so that it will at least add one new true ought-belief to A's beliefs if A takes it, that is, if A has n true ought-beliefs at t1 and takes the moral pill at t2, then she will have at least n+1 true ought-beliefs at t3.[Direct-pill account]
(2) The belief "A ought to phi" is true if and only if A can reason to this belief from what she already believes prior to her action. [Subjectivism]
(3) There are morally non-perfect agents A in whom the pill will incite ought-beliefs which they cannot reason to from what they already believe. [Causal influence hypothesis]
(4) There are morally non-perfect agents in whom the pill will incite at least one ought-belief which is true (by (1)) and which is false (by (2)). [Contradiction from 1,2,3]

As (4) is a contradiction, one of the premises must be denied. (2) is a controversial, but well defended claim. (3) follows from the sort of influence postulated by the direct-pill account. So this leaves giving up (or weakening) (1), the definition of the direct pill. Let me elaborate on this.

As a first response, we could weaken (1) so that it only spells out effectiveness-conditions for the pill, but then again the large class of agents referred to in (3), a class we especially want to make more moral, will not be affected by the pill, resulting in unwanted disjunctive recipes.

(2) is the most controversial assumption and I don't have space to defend it properly. However, others have done so with great rigor (see Dancy 2000, Gibbons 2010, Kiesewetter 2011, Robertson 2011, Scanlon 2008, Zimmerman 2008). In general, it seems plausible to me that subjectivism is the best solution for cases like the following: Rita, a doctor, faces the inevitable decision of giving a patient either medicine A or B. Rita thinks, taking everything she knows into account, A will kill the patient and B will cure him, but in fact the reverse is true. It appears strange to claim here that Rita ought to give A even though she thinks A will kill the patient.[3] My version of subjectivism is focused on whether Rita *can* reason to the conclusion that she ought to give A. If it follows from her knowledge and the evidence she can gather until the point of action that she ought to give A, then she ought to give A. I find this the most plausible construal of the truth-conditions of ought-beliefs given our everyday practice of justifying them by reference to their relation to our belief-system. The argument can be made to work with other versions of subjectivism too however. (2) can still be denied of course, if one has strong independent reasons for believing in objectivism. Yet one would then still face the question of how the direct pill would work. An objectivist would have to claim that the pill can somehow identify what the truths about oughts are, inciting exactly those beliefs that correspond to these oughts, which is certainly not a less implausible project to embark on.

So denial of (2) comes with a heavy load of commitments and further questions and is certainly not the first choice. This leaves (3).

But (3) follows from the conception of the direct pill. Supposedly, the directness of the pill consists in its purely causal influence on an agent's belief system. This way of bringing about mental states is, by definition, completely separate from whether the agent can reason to the state in question. One group of agents exemplifies this point rather well. Think of agents who have very few moral beliefs but good reasoning capacities. Such agents may have already reached every conclusion about what they ought to do they can reach given their moral beliefs. But they are not morally perfect agents by far. The pill will, by definition, incite true beliefs in those agents, but, by subjectivist standards, those beliefs will be false.

---

3. There is a temptation to think that there are several uses of "ought" in play here. Note that subjectivism is aimed at accounting for the Rita-case straightforwardly, without having to rely on strong claims about the ambiguity of "ought" which, even if true, would not settle the question about what Rita ought to do all things or "all oughts" considered.

A way to try to deny (3) may be to say that we should understand (1) so that the pill will *make it the case* that any agent A has at least one new ought-belief after taking it. In the case of the agents discussed above, the pill will then not only add new ought-beliefs, but all the other beliefs needed to make them true, most notably meta-beliefs about what follows from the newly added beliefs.

The first problem with the objection to (3) is that by the standards of subjectivism, it might still be true that agents *cannot* reason from what they know to the new ought-belief in rare cases where the agent has some small reasoning deficiency. So the new ought-belief might still be false.

The second problem with this objection is that it is unclear how we could imagine a pill having such precise and fine-tuned effects, especially if we keep in mind that it will have to incite different sets of beliefs for every different agent if subjectivism is true. The problem under discussion here – whether there is a non-disjunctive formula for engineering a moral pill – will reoccur at this level because we will need a general formula for making the pill incite in every agent exactly those beliefs and meta-beliefs that will make her new ought-beliefs true. But if subjectivism is true, the formula would seem to develop into a long, disjunctive list again, even if we keep the content of the relevant ought-belief constant.

The upshot of this discussion is that the direct pill will be impossible or ineffective given the truth of subjectivism.

The general conclusion for my guiding question is thus that the hope for finding *the* moral pill is dim. Ability pills leave unwilling agents unaffected and can only make them perform more morally right actions by means of manipulation. And manipulated agents will not be "morally better" in a sense that I find plausible. Direct pills may escape problems about lacking intentions to act morally, but given very plausible truth-conditions for ought-beliefs, they will be conceptually impossible (or ineffective). We could of course write a recipe as the disjunction of all the different ways *some* agents can become more moral. But this just seems to leave us where we started: that there are many different ways to make many different people more moral.[4]

---

4. I owe gratitude to all participants of the Kolloquium für Praktische Philosophie at Humboldt-Universität zu Berlin for many helpful comments and especially to Thomas Schmidt for providing me with the opportunity to present a version of this text at his Kolloquium. I am especially indebted to Berit Braun, Milena Bartholain, Stephanie Elsen and Razvan Sofroni for thorough discussion and most of all to Daniele Bruno, who also came up with the title. I would also like to thank Rita Schumacher.

References

Dancy, Jonathan 2000: *Practical Reality.* New York: Oxford University Press.
Gibbons, John 2010: "Things That Make Things Reasonable". *Philosophy and Phenomenological Research* 81(2), 335–61.
Kiesewetter, Benjamin 2011: "'Ought' and the Perspective of the Agent". *Journal for Ethics and Social Philosophy* 5(3), 1–24.
Pereboom, Derk 2001: *Living Without Free Will.* Cambridge: Cambridge University Press.
Robertson, Simon 2011: "Epistemic Constraints on Practical Normativity". *Synthese* 181, 81–106.
Scanlon, Thomas 2008: *Moral Dimensions: Permissibility, Meaning, Blame.* Cambridge, Mass.: Harvard University Press.
Zimmerman, Michael J. 2008: *Living with Uncertainty: The Moral Significance of Ignorance.* Cambridge: Cambridge University Press.

Wolfgang KÜNNE, *Epimenides und andere Lügner*. Frankfurt am Main: Klostermann Verlag. 2013. 173 S. ISBN: 978-3-465-04177-1

Eine der berühmtesten Paradoxien in der Philosophiegeschichte ist die sogenannte „Lügner-Antinomie". Die Forschung zu dieser faszinierenden Antinomie hat die Entwicklung der modernen Logik, Sprachphilosophie und Semantik entscheidend vorangetrieben und der formalen Analyse von Wahrheit, Falschheit, Selbstbezug, Anführung und metasprachlicher Rede wichtige neue Impulse verliehen. Unter einer „Lügner-Antinomie" wird in der gegenwärtigen Diskussion meist eine fatale logische Inkonsistenz verstanden, die durch einen Satz entsteht (den sogenannten „Lügner-Satz" oder kurz „Lügner"), der seine eigene Falschheit ausdrückt. Beispiele für „Lügner-Sätze" sind etwa die folgenden Sätze (1), (2) und (3):

(1) Dieser Satz ist falsch.
(2) Satz (2) ist falsch.
(3) <u>Der einzige auf dieser Seite unterstrichene Satz ist falsch.</u>

Die Sätze (1), (2) und (3) sind offensichtlich genau dann wahr, wenn sie falsch sind. Sind derartige „Lügner-Sätze" etwa im Rahmen einer klassischen, auf dem Bivalenzprinzip und dem Prinzip vom ausgeschlossenen Widerspruch beruhenden Logik formulierbar, so droht die *Inkonsistenz* dieser Logik – und damit ihre *Trivialisierung*, da in einer klassischen Logik aus einem Widerspruch jeder *beliebige* Satz ableitbar ist. Wenn eine Logik einfach alles abzuleiten gestattet, dann bedeutet das natürlich ihr Todesurteil. Doch wie kann man die „Lügner-Antinomie" vermeiden oder zumindest ihre dramatischen Konsequenzen eindämmen? Worin besteht die genaue formale Struktur von „Lügner-Sätzen", und welche logischen und semantischen Eigenschaften besitzen sie? Die Beantwortung dieser Fragen hat vor allem in der analytischen Philosophie des 20. (und 21.) Jahrhunderts eine regelrechte „Lügner-Industrie" heraufbeschworen, in der immer wieder neue Analysen des „Lügners" sowie Lösungs- oder Vermeidungsstrategien der „Lügner-Antinomie" entwickelt wurden. Die Antinomie erwies sich dabei jedoch als recht hartnäckig, da häufig vermeintliche Lösungsansätze neuen „Lügner-Varianten" (in Form sogenannter „verstärkter Lügner"[1]) zum Opfer fielen.

Die meisten gegenwärtigen Philosophinnen und Philosophen, die sich in logisch-systematischer Hinsicht mit der „Lügner-Antinomie" befassen, machen sich über deren genaue historische Ursprünge wenig Gedanken. Sie übernehmen den Begriff der „Lügner-Antinomie" oder des „Lügners" oft recht kritiklos. Als Quelle der „Lügner-Antinomie" gilt vielen die bereits in der Antike diskutierte vermeintlich paradoxe Situation, die dadurch entsteht, dass eine Person behauptet, „Ich lüge". Häufig wird hierbei auch auf (den Kreter) Epimenides verwiesen, der gesagt haben soll, dass alle Kreter lügen. Da jedoch diese „Lügner-Sätze" nicht dazu geeignet sind, eindeutige logische Widersprüche zu erzeugen, wird der „Lügner" heute meist ohne den semantisch, pragmatisch und sprechakttheoretisch vielschichtigen Begriff des Lügens formuliert. Auch ist der „Lügner" heute keine Person mehr, die z. B. behauptet zu lügen, sondern eben ein Satz, der seine eigene Falschheit ausdrückt.

Wolfgang Künne missfällt die gedankenlose Verwendung des Ausdrucks „Lügner-Antinomie" bzw. „Lügner" in der zeitgenössischen philosophischen Diskussion. Für ihn trägt die „Lügner-Antinomie" ihren Namen zu Unrecht. In seiner Studie *Epimenides und andere Lügner* werden anhand zahlreicher historisch-philologischer Belege verschiedene Varianten der „Lügner-Antinomie" unter die Lupe genommen – vornehmlich aus der Perspektive Bernard Bolzanos. Auch werden in einem eigenen Kapitel logisch-semantische Eigentümlichkeiten paradoxienfreier selbstbezüglicher Sätze behandelt.

Das Buch besteht neben einer kurzen Einleitung aus drei Kapiteln sowie sechs Anhängen. Historische Abbildungen einiger der Hauptprotagonisten der Abhandlung illustrieren zudem den Text.

Im ersten Kapitel werden zunächst Bolzanos Überlegungen zu einem Trugschluss *(pseudómenos)* erörtert, der auf Aristoteles' Einteilung der Trugschlussarten in den *Sophistische[n] Widerlegungen* zurückgeht. Aristoteles verweist hier u. a. auf eine Trugschlussform, die später als *fallacia secundum quid et simpliciter* bezeichnet wurde – ein Fehlschluss also, der durch „Weglassen einer nötigen Einschränkung" entsteht (Künne 2013, 16). Bolzanos Version dieses Trugschlusses beruht auf einem Argument, das von der Möglichkeit ausgeht, dass ein Lügner gestehen kann, ein Lügner zu sein. Wenn nun aber ein Lügner gesteht, ein Lügner zu sein, dann spricht er offenkundig die Wahrheit. Woraus nun aber folgt, dass es möglich ist, dass ein Lügner die Wahrheit spricht. Mit der zusätzlichen Annahme, dass ein Lügner niemals die Wahrheit spricht, folgt nun die widersprüchliche Aussage, dass es möglich ist, dass ein Lügner kein Lügner ist. Dieses Argument wird von Künne als der „Geständige Lügner" bezeichnet und sowohl in modallogischer wie in „entmodalisierender" Version rekonstruiert (siehe Künne 20f.). Die widersprüchliche Konklusion im Argument des „Geständigen Lügners" stellt nun aber keine Antinomie dar, sondern beruht, wie bereits Bolzano feststellte, auf einer falschen Annahme in Bezug auf den Begriff des Lügens bzw. des Lügners. Es handelt sich hier um die Annahme, dass ein Lügner niemals die Wahrheit spricht. Selbstverständlich kann jemand, der schlechthin ein Lügner ist, in punktuellen Fällen auch einmal etwas Wahres sagen. Außerdem, so Künne, kann auch eine wahre Behauptung eine Lüge sein, nämlich dann, wenn der Lügner der irrigen Auffassung ist, dass die Behauptung falsch ist. Die Überlegungen zu Bolzanos „Geständigem Lügner" führen Künne zur Frage, was eigentlich eine Lüge ist. Auch hier setzt er bei Bolzanos Explikation des Begriffs der Lüge an, wonach eine Lüge stets mit einer Täuschungsabsicht verbunden ist und aus einer Behauptung besteht, die das lügende Subjekt selbst für falsch hält.

Nach diesem Exkurs zur Begriffsanalyse der Lüge folgen Erörterungen zu vier Darstellungen der „Antinomie des Lügners": 1. die von Cicero stammende Darstellung, die als eine der ältesten Überlieferungen der „Lügner-Antinomie" gilt, 2. die Version von Alexander von Aphrodisias, 3. die Variante der „Lügner-Antinomie" in einem vermutlich von Michael von Ephesos geschriebenen Kommentar zu den *Sophistischen Widerlegungen* und 4. Bertrand Russells Formulierung des „Lügners" in der Einleitung zu den *Principia Mathematica* in Form eines Sprechers, der sagt, dass er (jetzt gerade) lüge.

In seiner Erläuterung zu Ciceros Darstellung der „Lügner-Antinomie" unterscheidet Künne zwei Übersetzungsvarianten, die keineswegs gleichbedeutend sind (siehe Künne 2013, 38):

(L) Ich lüge.
(F) Ich sage etwas Falsches.

Zwar ist die Version (L) diejenige, die als Namenspatronin für die „Lügner-Antinomie" herhalten musste, allerdings besitzt, so Künne, nur die Version (F) antinomisches Potential. Die „Lügner-Antinomie" müsste daher seiner Meinung nach besser und treffender als *Antinomie der Falschheit* oder kurz *F-Antinomie* bezeichnet werden. Wie bereits erwähnt, kann nach Künne jemand lügen und dennoch (ohne es zu wollen) etwas Wahres sagen, und man kann natürlich etwas Falsches behaupten, ohne dabei zu lügen. Version (L) ist daher gar nicht antinomisch. Die Version (F), so argumentiert Künne, führt zudem nur in einer reflexiven Deutung zu einer Antinomie, welche etwa durch den folgenden Satz (F_{refl}) besser zum Ausdruck kommt (siehe Künne 2013, 47):

(F_{refl}) Ich sage mit diesem ($\leftrightarrows$) Satz etwas Falsches. (Das Pfeilsymbol steht hierbei für die reflexive Deutung, wonach das Denotat der demonstrativen Kennzeichnung eben der Satz (F_{refl}) selbst ist.)

Russell, aber auch viele andere bedeutende Philosophen des 20. Jahrhunderts wie W. V. O. Quine oder Saul Kripke, verweisen zudem auf eine Stelle im Neuen Testament als wichtige historische Quelle der „Lügner-Antinomie". Dort wird im Brief des Apostels Paulus an Titus ein Kreter zitiert, der (neben anderen unschönen Dingen über seine kretischen Landsleute) behauptet, dass alle Kreter lügen. Dass es sich bei diesem „kretischen Nestbeschmutzer" um den Philosophen und berühmten Seher Epimenides aus Knossos handelt, wie oft behauptet wird, ist, so Künne, jedoch äußerst fragwürdig.[2] Die Bezeichnung „Paradox of Epimenides", wie sie sich z. B. bei Quine findet, ist daher schon im Hinblick auf den vermeintlichen Namensgeber dieser „Paradoxie" unglücklich. Schlimmer wiegt jedoch für Künne, dass der „Epimenides" genauso wenig wie der „Lügner" zu einer Antinomie Anlass gibt. Selbst wenn man im Dictum des Kreters den Begriff des Lügens tilgt und diesen durch den (natürlich nicht gleichbedeutenden) Begriff des *Falschbehauptens* ersetzt, so folgt lediglich, dass die Behauptung des Kreters („Alle Kreter behaupten nur Falsches") nicht wahr sein kann und es somit mindestens eine andere (d. h. eine von der Behauptung des Kreters verschiedene) Aussage eines Kreters geben muss, die nicht falsch ist (siehe Künne 2013, 56). Nur wenn man, wie es u. a. Russell und Quine getan haben, zusätzlich annimmt, dass es keine andere Aussage eines Kreters geben kann, die wahr ist (was aber natürlich ziemlich absurd und irreal anmutet), erlangt man eine Antinomie – die Künne als *Kretische Antinomie* bezeichnet.

Künne widmet sich im zweiten Kapitel Bolzanos Erörterung der „Lügner-Antinomie" (bzw. F-Antinomie) in Girolamo Savonarolas *Compendium logicae* (von 1492). Für Savonarola ist eine reflexive Äußerung der Form „Dies ist falsch" ein Beispiel für ein *Insolubile* – ein *Unlösbares* in Gestalt eines „sich selbst zerstörenden Satzes" (siehe Künne 2013, 76). Künne diskutiert die Version der Antinomie von Savonarola in Gestalt des folgenden reflexiven Satzes (ψ):

(ψ) Die Proposition, die dieser (⇆) Satz ausdrückt, ist falsch.

Es lässt sich leicht einsehen, dass (ψ) genau dann wahr ist, wenn (ψ) falsch ist. Savonarola versucht die Antinomie nun dadurch aufzulösen bzw. erst gar nicht entstehen zu lassen, dass er (ψ) sowie reflexive „Sätze" der Art „Dieser (⇆) Satz ist falsch" gar nicht als Sätze anerkennt. Er zählt somit zu den Anhängern der sogenannten *Nullifizierer*, nach denen „Lügner-Sätze" (ich sollte natürlich besser „F-Sätze" sagen) bloße Scheinsätze sind. Gegen die Strategie der „Nullifizierer" lässt sich jedoch, so Künne, u. a. einwenden, dass sich manche Sätze erst aufgrund unglücklicher äußerer Umstände als antinomisch erweisen. Behauptet etwa ein Sprecher „Die Proposition, die durch meine letzten Worte ausgedrückt wird, ist falsch" (Künne 2013, 85), so müssten „Nullifizierer" kontraintuitiverweise dieser Aussage nachträglich den Satzstatus entziehen, wenn z. B. der Sprecher, ohne etwas Weiteres zu sagen, nach dieser Behauptung dahinscheidet …

Während die ersten beiden Kapitel der Geschichte der „Lügner-Antinomie" gewidmet sind, erörtert Künne im dritten Kapitel einige semantische Eigentümlichkeiten selbstbezüglicher Sätze. Diese Eigentümlichkeiten sind zwar in der gegenwärtigen Diskussion bekannt und werden in formalen Logiken, die (paradoxienfrei) selbstbezügliche Satzstrukturen zu formulieren erlauben, berücksichtigt, dennoch sind die Zusammenstellung und Diskussion der spezifischen Eigenschaften von paradoxienfreiem Selbstbezug und der möglichen Fallstricke, in die man sich begibt, wann man diese Eigenschaften nicht beachtet, interessant und instruktiv. Auch wenn viele F-Antinomien selbstbezüglich sind, ist doch der Selbstbezug weder hinreichend noch notwendig für eine Antinomie. So ist etwa weder der von Platon zum Zeitpunkt t geäußerte Satz (π) noch der von Sokrates zum selben Zeitpunkt t geäußerte Satz (σ) selbstbezüglich (siehe Künne 2013, 93):

(π) Was Sokrates jetzt gerade sagt, ist wahr.
(σ) Was Platon jetzt gerade sagt, ist falsch.

Dennoch erzeugen sie zusammen eine F-Antinomie. Auch gibt es durchaus selbstbezügliche Sätze, die keineswegs antinomisch sind, wie den Satz „Dieser (⇆) Satz besteht aus sechs Wörtern".

Da in selbstbezüglichen Sätzen der verwendete Satz auch erwähnt wird und daher in Form eines logischen Individuenausdrucks ebenfalls als Satzsubjekt fungiert, entstehen gewisse Besonderheiten bei der *Negation* eines selbstbezüglichen Satzes. So sind natürlich die folgenden Sätze (S3) und (S4) (siehe Künne 2013, 97) keine Negationen voneinander:

(S3) Die Anzahl der Wörter, aus denen dieser (⇆) Satz besteht, ist zwölf.
(S4) Die Anzahl der Wörter, aus denen dieser (⇆) Satz besteht, ist nicht zwölf.

In (S3) fungiert „Die Anzahl der Wörter, aus denen dieser (⇆) Satz besteht, ist zwölf" als Satzsubjekt, dem das Prädikat, aus zwölf Wörtern zu bestehen, zugeschrieben wird. In (S4) ist „Die Anzahl der Wörter, aus denen dieser (⇆) Satz besteht, ist nicht zwölf" das Satzsubjekt, von dem ausgesagt wird, dass es nicht aus zwölf Wörtern besteht. Beide Behauptungen sind daher falsch: Das Satzsubjekt in (S3) besteht aus elf und das in (S4) aus zwölf Wörtern.[3]

Ähnliche Eigentümlichkeiten ergeben sich auch bei *Deduktionen* mit selbstbezüglichen Sätzen (siehe Künne 2013, 102–106). Auch ist bei der Übersetzung selbstbezüglicher Sätze Vorsicht geboten. So kann man natürlich nicht den Satz „Dies (⇆) ist ein deutscher Satz" mit dem Satz „This (⇆) is a German sentence" ins Englische übersetzen – sondern mit dem Satz „This (⇆) is an English sentence".

Wer sich für die Geschichte der „Lügner-Antinomie" interessiert, wird in Künnes lehrreichem Buch viele neue und spannende Entdeckungen machen. Die vielen (manchmal, um den Lesefluss nicht zu beeinträchtigen, in Fußnoten verbannten) historischen Details sowie die zahlreichen philosophischen, literarischen und bibelkundlichen Bezüge sind informativ und mit einem gewissen Unterhaltungswert zu lesen, auch wenn (oder vielleicht gerade weil) der Stil einer streng akademisch argumentierenden Abhandlung an einigen Stellen durchbrochen wird. Wer allerdings eine Diskussion zu den verschiedenen modernen Ansätzen oder gar einen eigenen Beitrag zur logisch-semantischen Analyse und Lösung der Antinomie erwartet, wird enttäuscht.

Eine kleinere Schwachstelle des Buches liegt vielleicht darin, dass manchmal zu stark auf die historische Dimension und auf die Perspektive Bolzanos fokussiert wird. So bleiben etwa in der Diskussion zum Begriff des Lügens bzw. der Lüge viele der einschlägigen gegenwärtigen Untersuchungen aus der Linguistik, Sprachphilosophie und Ethik außen vor. Manche der im Buch behaupteten notwendigen Eigenschaften des Lügens werden von einigen Autorinnen und Autoren der aktuellen Diskussion gerade in Frage gestellt. So wird die für Künne zentrale These, dass das Lügen nicht immer damit verbunden zu sein braucht, etwas Falsches zu behaupten, und dass allein die Überzeugung des Sprechers entscheidend sei, etwa von Thomas Carson (Carson 2006, 2010) oder William Lycan (Lycan 2006) bestritten. Auch erweitern einige moderne Autorinnen und Autoren die Definition der Lüge dahingehend, dass auch Implikaturen (das, was über das Gesagte hinaus eigentlich mit einer Äußerung gemeint ist) zum Lügen eingesetzt werden können (siehe z. B. Meibauer 2005, 2014) – was Künne jedoch offenbar bestreitet (siehe Künne 2013, 31f.). Zudem gibt es zahlreiche Analysen des Lügenbegriffs, wie Künne ja auch zugibt, die (im Unterschied zu Bolzano) auf die Täuschungsabsicht des Sprechers als notwendige Bedingung für Lügen verzichten (siehe z. B. Carson 2006, 2010, Fallis 2009, Sorensen 2007, 2010). Es gibt nämlich viele Fälle, in denen es dem Gegenüber sehr wohl bekannt ist (und der Sprecher auch weiß, dass dies dem Gegenüber bekannt ist), dass der Sprecher lügt. Der Sprecher lügt in diesen Fällen (z. B. aus Angst vor Strafe oder Rache oder aus Zwang), obwohl er nicht die Absicht hat zu täuschen. Dennoch, so argumentiert z. B. Jennifer Lackey (siehe Lackey 2013), versucht der Lügende auch in diesen Fällen bestimmte Informationen vor dem Gegenüber zu verbergen – Informationen, die explizit ausgesprochen ihn offiziell als Lügner ausweisen würden und negative Konsequenzen für ihn zur Folge hätten. Der Sprechakt des Lügens ist (im Unterschied etwa zum Sprechakt des Versprechens) daher selbst bei nicht vorhandener Täuschungsabsicht des Sprechers niemals mit einem Hinweis auf die illokutionäre Kraft des Sprechakts verbunden. Während man selbstverständlich sagen kann, „Hiermit verspreche ich, dass p", käme es, wie Jörg Meibauer treffend feststellt, einem „illokutionären Selbstmord" gleich (siehe Meibauer 2005, 1374), würde der Lügende sagen: „Ich lüge hiermit (bzw. es ist eine Lüge), dass p."[4]

Vor diesem Hintergrund der Debatte um das Verhältnis von Lügen und Täuschen scheint die „Lügner-Antinomie" in ihrer ursprünglichsten Form, d. h. in Gestalt einer Person, die behauptet, „Ich lüge (gerade jetzt)", genau einen solchen „illokutionären Selbstmord" zu begehen. Zudem widerspricht dieser „Lügner" anderen wesentlichen Eigenschaften der Lüge bzw. des Lügens. Auch schon aus diesem Grund tun die modernen Philosophinnen und Philosophen gut daran, den Begriff des Lügens aus ihren Formulierungen der „Lügner-Antinomie" zu verbannen. Ob sich jedoch der Ausdruck „F-Antinomie" durchsetzen wird, ist allerdings zweifelhaft, wie auch Künne etwas resigniert feststellt. Der Ausdruck „Lügner-Antinomie" bzw. „Lügner" hat sich schon zu sehr in den Köpfen festgesetzt. Dass er aber nur noch ein (die Antinomie der Falschheit) denotierender und keineswegs beschreibender oder konnotierender Ausdruck ist, wird man spätestens nach der Lektüre von Künnes Buch wissen.

Elke BRENDEL
Universität Bonn

1. In der meist englischsprachigen Literatur werden diese Varianten der „Lügner-Antinomie" oft als *strengthened liar*, *extended liar* oder auch als *revenge liar* tituliert.
2. Näheres zu Epimenides findet sich auch im Anhang III.
3. Der Doppelpfeil ($\leftrightarrows$) zählt dabei natürlich nicht zu den Wörtern des Satzes.
4. Allerdings ist es natürlich möglich, dass man später kleinlaut zugeben kann, dass man mit einer bestimmten Äußerung gelogen habe.

Literatur

Carson, Thomas L. 2006: „The Definition of Lying". *Noûs* 40, 284–306.
Carson, Thomas L. 2010: *Lying and Deception. Theory and Practice*. Oxford: Oxford University Press.
Fallis, Don 2009: „What is Lying?". *The Journal of Philosophy* 106, 29–56.
Lackey, Jennifer 2013: „Lies and Deception: An Unhappy Divorce". *Analysis* 73, 236–248.
Lycan, William G. 2006: „On the Gettier Problem Problem". In: Stephen Hetherington (Hg.), *Epistemology Futures*. Oxford: Clarendon Press, 148–168.
Meibauer, Jörg 2005: „Lying and Falsely Implicating". *Journal of Pragmatics* 37, 1373–1399.
Meibauer, Jörg 2014: *Lying at the Semantics-Pragmatics Interface*. Boston/Berlin: Walter de Gruyter.
Sorensen, Roy 2007: „Bald-Faced Lies! Lying Without the Intent to Deceive". *Pacific Philosophical Quarterly* 88, 251–264.
Sorensen, Roy 2010: „Knowledge-lies". *Analysis* 70, 608–615.

Denis FISETTE and Guillaume FRÉCHETTE (eds.), *Themes from Brentano*. Amsterdam-New York, NY: Rodopi. 2013. 530 pp. ISBN 9789042037427

As Guillaume Fréchette remarks in the introductory essay to this volume, Brentano has the reputation of being both very visible as a philosopher and, in a sense, almost completely invisible. Most in the analytic tradition recognise him for his view that intentionality is the mark of the mental, and recognise the impact of this doctrine, for good or ill, on subsequent work in the philosophy of mind. For many their knowledge will probably stop there. They will see Brentano as someone with insights that have had significant impact, but not as someone who had developed views worth knowing about. Philosophers in the continental tradition are likely to have similar reactions. Brentano may have rediscovered the importance of intentionality but it is to Husserl and phenomenology that we turn for its mature reconceptualization. Brentano was someone who found a central place for the idea of intentionality but didn't run with it (unlike his student Husserl and unlike the phenomenological movement more generally), and didn't recognise its rich metaphysical significance (unlike his student Meinong). In short, Brentano was influential as an initiator of important ideas (influential enough for him to be selected as the target of Quine's attack on the intentional idiom in the 1950s), but little more.

As Fréchette also points out, this description is somewhat of a caricature. In fact, Brentano's work was widely known in the 20th century, both through the work of his students a number of whom, like Stumpf and Marty, continued to respond to his ideas, and through the work of philosophers like Chisholm who introduced Brentano's work to American philosophy. The idea of Brentano's invisibility has more to do with mid- to late-20th century philosophical fashion; philosophers haven't wanted to throw him more than a glance because they have preferred the way others worked with some of the notions he (re-)discovered. In Fréchette's words, Brentano's invisibility "has more to do with his marginalization from both the analytic and continental philosophy of the 1950s, as a mere 'forerunner of the phenomenological movement', a 'precursor of Husserl', or, as Ryle calls him …, the 'disgusted grandfather of phenomenology" (14). This is unlikely to be the whole truth, I suspect. It is also true that Brentano failed to publish material, especially lectures, that would have increased exposure to his ideas; and as Thomas Binder points out in his contribution to this volume, too little is known, even at this stage, about the full range of his unpublished writings.

That, very roughly, is the philosophical-sociological background to *Themes from Brentano*. The book is an attempt to highlight important themes in Brentano's work, written by a range of experts on Brentano's philosophy, both to let the philosophical community reacquaint itself with the rich mother lode that has given us Brentanian ideas and also to show how, and why, these ideas continue to exert their influence.

The editors have chosen a coarse-grained characterization of the themes they focus on: i) the epistemological priority of inner over outer perception, ii) Brentano's conception of intentionality as the mark of the mental, and iii) his ontological conception of the mind and the world as mereological structures. These themes play central roles in different Brentanian doctrines. The first, for example, plays a central role in his theory of evidence but also his theory of consciousness. The second affects his conception of perception, sensations, emotions, cognition and valuation. The third is in a way the most wide-ranging: it underlies his ontology and philosophy of mind, but also his ethics and logic. They are not themes, Fréchette stresses, that constitute the work of a systematic philosopher in the classical sense (14). Instead, Brentano is best viewed as a methodologically distinctive figure who wrote at a time of opposing "-isms" (idealism, empiricism, positivism, etc), someone who favored instead a rigorous analytic and descriptive approach to philosophical problems, in the manner of a good scientist rather than a foundational system-builder. Viewed this way, Brentano's themes appear as systematic features of his thought, worked on and elaborated through a systematic application of this methodology.

The first three sections of the book are loosely devoted to each of the themes, while the last two sections have an after-Brentano focus. There clearly was no particular brief the authors were requested to follow, and so we have some chapters whose express purpose is to clarify Brentano's actual views, including their historical background, while others revisit Brentanian themes in light of contemporary views and concepts that can often be traced to Brentano. Uriah Kriegel begins section 1 with an excellent example of this second approach. 'Brentano's Most Striking Thesis: No Representation without Self-Representation' is a nuanced exploration of Brentano's self-representational account of consciousness, with Kriegel's own version— in brief, "Every paradigmatic token of representations-of is also a representation-to"—a logically sophisticated reformulation of Brentano's view. Johannes Brandl's chapter 'What is Pre-reflective Awareness?' is more speculative. It offers an interpretation of Brentano's distinction between inner perception and inner observation to argue that Brentano had a conception of pre-reflective awareness (a notion that, in its current form, is usually said to have emerged in Husserl and the phenomenological tradition) that is more sophisticated than many other accounts. Rounding out the discussions of the first theme is Mark Textor's chapter on 'Unity without Self', which is a critical exposition of Brentano's neglected view that among the marks of the mental is a particular kind of unity. Without endorsing the account, Textor argues that Brentano's conception of this unity is on the surface superior to competitors like Hume's bundle theory, especially when it is understood with the help of his student Carl Stumpf's notion of fusion.

Section 2, on 'Varieties of intentionality', begins with Fréchette's excellent paper 'Brentano's Thesis (Revisited),' which argues that Brentano's work shows evidence of a distinction between the content and object of the intentional relation and, relatedly, a distinction between two very different features of intentionality: inclusion and directedness. This allows Fréchette to develop an answer to certain objections from Brentano's students regarding the intentionality of sensations, and allows him to criticize Chisholm's influential understanding of Brentano's intentionality thesis (along the way denying that Brentano ever found a satisfactory solution to the problem of true negative existential judgments). The second paper, by Arkadiusz Chrudzimski, situates Brentano's work relative to Aristotle, and argues that, contrary to a common perception and Brentano's own repeated assurances, his indebtedness to Aristotle was more in the way the latter did philosophy, as a close look at his various accounts of intentionality shows that there are "formidable" structural differences between his theory of immanent objects and Aristotle's view of sense-perception.

Very different is Laurent Cessalli's 'Marty's Intentionalist Theory of Meaning', which discusses Anton Marty's use of Brentano's ideas to give an account of meaning in terms of intentions: a speaker's primary intention to influence someone else's inner life and a secondary intention to indicate his own inner life. This paper was a revelation. Although Marty's theory is very different from Grice's intentionalist theory of meaning, there are intriguing comparisons to be made, and Cessalli does a good job showing the power of the approach. The final paper in this second section on intentionality is Matjaž Portč's paper on 'Phenomenology of Intentionality'. Like Brandl's paper in section 1, it is more speculative than most of the other papers since it relates directly to a current view—that intentionality has a phenomenology, a core thesis of the phenomenal intentionality program —which doesn't seem to have direct Brentanian roots, even though it looks as if Brentano ought to have things to say about it. While one might dispute some of what Portč says, I think his reflections successfully show that Brentano's perspective on intentionality is detailed and rich enough to allow one to ask 'What would Brentano have thought?'

The final thematic section concerns ontology and metaphysics. Heading the section is Werner Sauer's paper 'Being as the True', alongside Chrudzimski's paper the only paper in the book that looks at the historical precedents of Brentano's work. In his deep and carefully argued paper, Sauer proposes that Brentano's development of the Aristotelian doctrine of being as the True resulted from his reading of Aquinas's commentary on Aristotle's *Metaphysics*, in which being as the True *seems* to be interpreted in terms of the existential 'is': precisely the interpretation Brentano then adopted. Sauer points out that in his reistic phase Brentano came to see this as an error that he attributes to Aquinas, not Aristotle. The second paper of the section is Wilhelm Baumgartner's 'Franz Brentano's Mereology'. Formal mereology is an area that has become central to debates in analytic metaphysics and ontology (it even touches the philosophy of mathematics), and this paper should be required reading for anyone interested in the history of the field and the pivotal role that Brentano plays in it. Baumgartner describes the many ways in which Brentano put the idea of part-whole relations to work, in areas as varied as metaphysics and ontology, psychology, and even the history of philosophy. Rounding off this section is Susan Gabriel's interesting 'Brentano at the Intersection of Psychology, Ontology and the Good', which explores the way Brentano uses mereology during his reistic period to attempt to solve the theological problem of evil, an approach that shows Brentano as "a systematic philosopher with the big picture always in mind" (247). Gabriel applauds Brentano's attempt at theodicy, but what value readers place on this attempt will no doubt depend on their assessment of his reism. Gabriel herself claims that reism is the logical result of a thoroughgoing commitment to the epistemic priority of the *cogito* (the first theme explored in the book), but that will strike many readers as at best doubtful (and it doesn't make the reism any more plausible).

There is much to admire in this first thematic part of the book (including the editors' useful introductions). In a nice touch, the editors extend the notion of 'themes from Brentano' to include two further sections that involve elements of a rather different kind. Both deal with 'the posterity of Brentano's philosophy', as Fréchette calls it. The first, which possibly began as an attempt to find a common home for contributions that specifically dealt with Brentano's account of feelings, sensations, and emotions, is thematized as being about the legacy of Brentano's account, in particular the involvement of members of Brenato's School, in their ongoing engagement with his account and the changes it underwent. The papers in this section include Olivier Massin's paper 'The Intentionality of Pleasure', which (guardedly) attributes a form of hedonic intentionalism to Brentano, and then uses Brentano's own objections to the theories of Hamilton and Stumpf to argue for the superiority of such a Brentanian view. The two remaining papers are even more centred on the critical contribution that Stumpf made to the debate. In 'Mixed Feelings', Denis Fisette argues that Stumpf's theory of emotions can be regarded as an attempt to reconcile Brentano's hedonic intentionalism with James's sensualism, drawing on the rich correspondence between Brentano and Stumpf to do so. The last paper in the section is Ricardo Martinelli's 'Stumpf and Brentano on Tonal Fusion', which describes the disagreement between Brentano and Stumpf on tonal fusion, and along the way very clearly demonstrates the versatility of Brentano's framework in allowing a variety of different ways in which to approach sensory and tonal perception.

Posterity in this section has focused on the way others, particularly students, engaged with Brentano's account of feelings and sensations. The final section of the book is on posterity in a more general sense. It contains Thomas Binder's 'There and back Again: an Updated History of Franz Brentano's Unpublished Papers', as well as some manuscripts from his Nachlass: the text of a 1890 lecture on 'Modern Errors concerning the Knowledge of the Laws of Inference' and the manuscript 'Abstraction and Relation', the latter accompanied by part of Brentano's correspondence with his student Anton Marty on the topic of relations (all are presented in both the original German and English translation).

The decision to include this section should be applauded. First of all, Binder's careful history is a remarkably moving document on how the vicissitudes of history have determined how little we know of Brentano's unpublished works. As Binder puts it, "we still do not know what Brentano has really written"—to date there is no complete edition of his unpublished papers that meets modern text-critical standards (370). (In comparison, and despite formidable obstacles, Husserl's Nachlass had it easy.) Binder suggests that this fact may provide "some of the external reasons which may have contributed negatively to the impact of Brentano's philosophy" (370). Secondly, the correspondence with Marty not only gives interesting insights into the way Brentano philosophises, but also contains some nice human touches: it records his pleasure at the favorable way his views were received by a certain philosopher, for example (and thinks this bodes well for their impact when that person gets his professorship; 462); it also contains some marvellously blistering comments on Stumpf, with whom he had fallen out (460).

I warmly recommend this book. It is an excellent work and one whose time has come. Binder's note of pessimism nothwithstanding (370), one can only hope that there will be many other books on Brentano to follow. We should not begrudge Brentano's students, Husserl and Meinong in particular, the fame and attention their views have garnered, but given the Brentanian background to their views and given the depth of Brentano's many contributions to philosophy, it is deeply unfortunate that his work has not received anywhere near the same attention. This book will help both to reduce Brentano's "invisibility" and advance the much needed rehabilitation of Brentano as one of the great philosophers of the second half of the 19th century and the beginning of the 20th century.

Fred KROON
University of Auckland